ROBERT ADAM'S LONDON

ROBERT ADAM'S LONDON

FRANCES SANDS

Produced in conjunction with an exhibition of the same title
at Sir John Soane's Museum (30 November 2016 – 11 March 2017)

With thanks to Colin Thom for consultation and peer review

Archaeopress Publishing Ltd
Gordon House
276 Banbury Road
Oxford OX2 7ED
www.archaeopress.com

ISBN 978 1 78491 462 2
ISBN 978 1 78491 463 9 (e-Pdf)

Text and images © Sir John Soane's Museum, 2016, unless otherwise indicated

Cover: Adam office, design for the ceiling for the glass drawing room at Northumberland House, 1770. SM Adam volume 11/33. Photograph: Geremy Butler

SIR JOHN
SOANE'S
MUSEUM
LONDON

Printed in England by Oxuniprint, Oxford
This book is available direct from Archaeopress or from our website www.archaeopress.com

Contents

List of Figures

Foreword

To complement his 'academy of architecture', Sir John Soane acquired the 8,000-strong Adam office drawings collection in 1833. Complete with a further 1,000 drawings from the Adam brothers' Grand Tours, this collection is thought to comprise over 80% of the surviving Adam drawings in the world, and has become an important focus for the study of eighteenth-century architectural history. Since 1998 the collection has been the subject of scholarly cataloguing projects. First, Alan Tait catalogued the Adam Grand Tour collection, and Frances Sands has been working on the Adam office drawings since 2010. This continuing project has resulted in the attribution of 1,500 previously unidentified drawings, contributing both to academic study and conservation works. The entire collection has been photographed, thanks to the generous support of the Leon Levy Foundation, and is available for consultation on the Soane Museum's Collections Online website.

One of the most prolific architects in Britain, Robert Adam produced more designs for London than anywhere else. This book assembles the stories of a great many of his commissions and speculative projects in the capital city, and uses the Adam drawings to illustrate the architect's intentions and achievements. The book is published alongside an exhibition at the Soane Museum of the same title. I would like to thank my colleagues at the Soane Museum for their work on both the exhibition and this book, particularly Frances Sands, who has made this project her own, Jo Tinworth, Sue Palmer, John Bridges, Lorraine Bryant and Helen Dorey. Moreover, I would like to express my thanks to Iain Gordon Brown for his support of the Adam drawings project in the capacity of consultant, and also to Colin Thom, Senior Historian at the Survey of London, who has been extremely generous with his time and expertise in reviewing this book.

Bruce Boucher
Director, Sir John Soane's Museum

Map of London

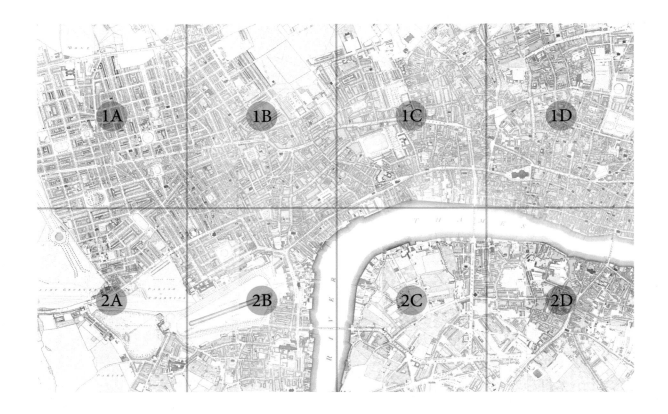

Richard Horwood, *Plan of the Cities of London and Westminster the Borough of Southwark, and parts adjoining shewing every house*, 1792–99, detail. Reproduced from the London Topographical Society facsimile, 1966, by courtesy of the Cushing Memorial Library and Archives, Texas A&M University

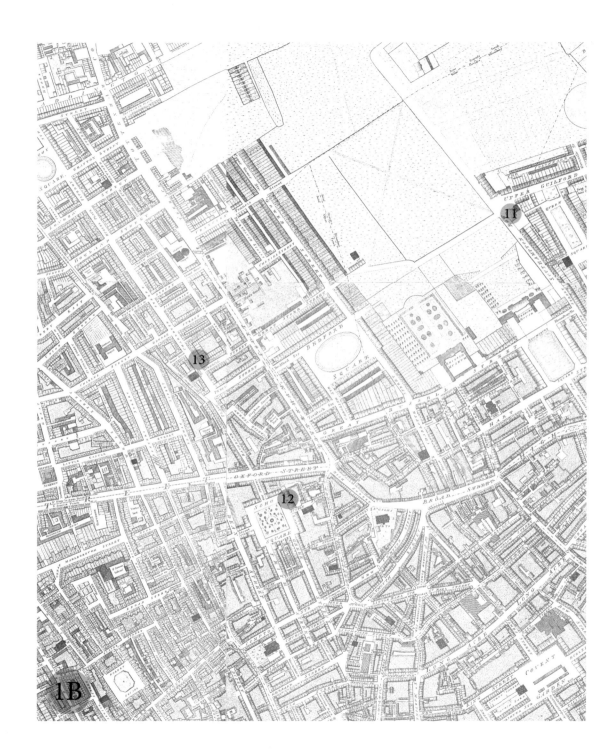

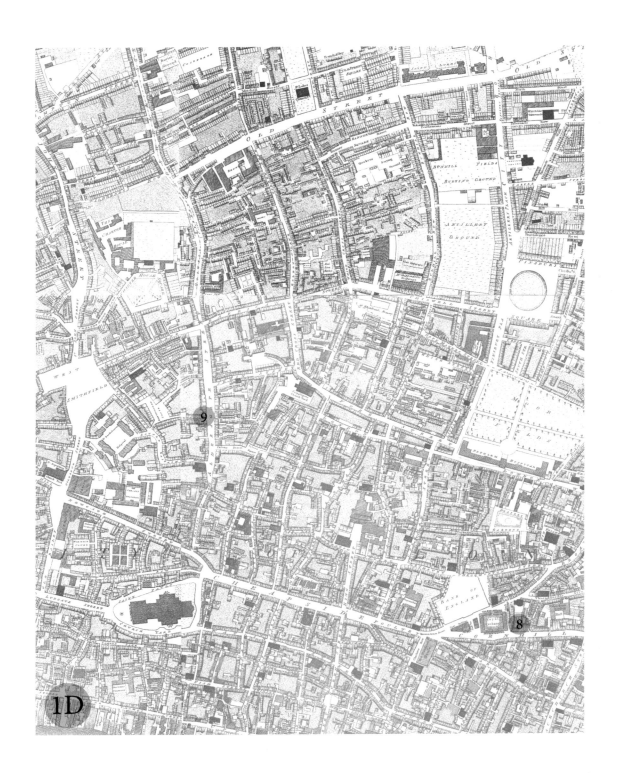

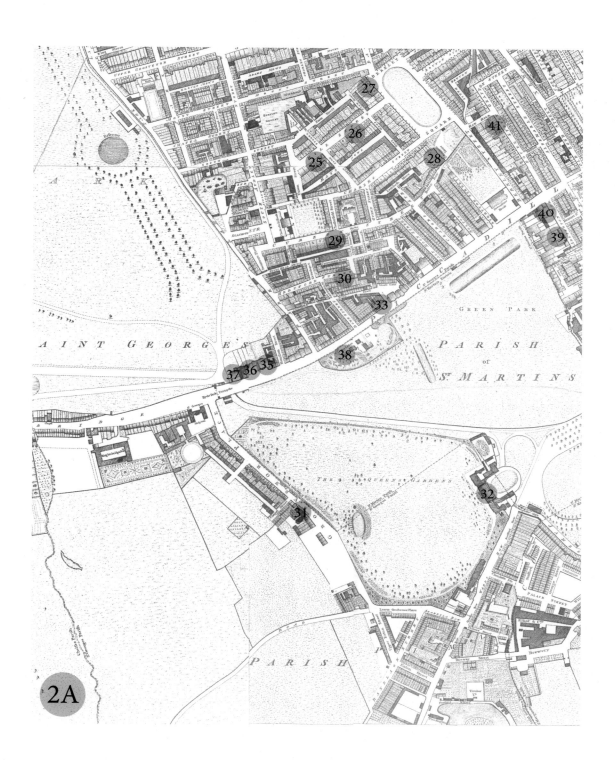

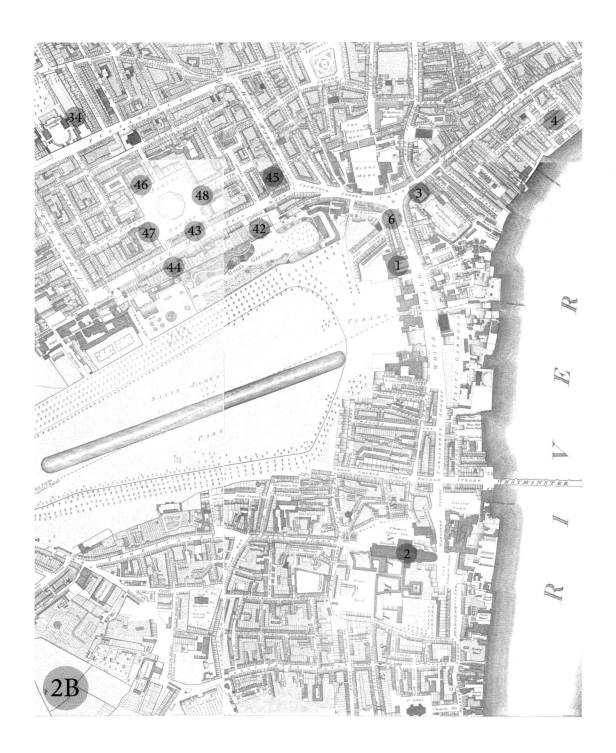

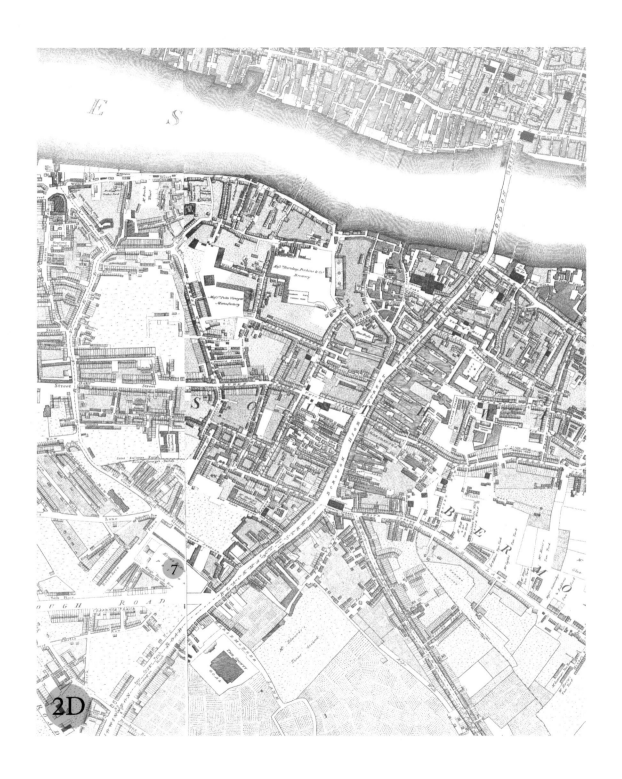

Key to Map

1. Admiralty, Whitehall (2B)
2. Westminster Abbey (2B)
3. Northumberland House, Strand (2B)
4. Adelphi (2B)
5. Theatre Royal, Drury Lane (1C)
6. Drummond's Bank, Charing Cross (2B)
7. King's Bench Prison, Southwark (2D)
8. Lloyd's Coffee House, Freeman's Court, Cornhill (1D)
9. 152 Aldersgate Street (1D)
10. Lincoln's Inn (1C)
11. Bolton House, Southampton Row (1B)
12. 20 Soho Square (1B)
13. 9 Charlotte Street (1B)
14. Mansfield Street (1A)
15. Portland House, New Cavendish Street (1A)
16. Portland Place (1A)
17. Clerk House, Duchess Street (1A)
18. Chandos House, Queen Anne Street (1A)
19. 20 Portman Square (1A)
20. 21 Portman Square (1A)
21. 41 Portman Square (1A)
22. 18 Grosvenor Square (1A)
23. 23 Grosvenor Square (1A)
24. 75 Lower Grosvenor Street (1A)
25. 23 Hill Street (2A)
26. 31 Hill Street (2A)
27. 15 Berkeley Square (2A)
28. Lansdowne House, Berkeley Square (2A)
29. 30 Curzon Street (2A)
30. 10 Hertford Street (2A)
31. Lock Hospital, Grosvenor Place (2A)
32. Buckingham House (2A)
33. Coventry House, 29 Piccadilly (2A)
34. 147 Piccadilly (2B)
35. Piccadilly at Hyde Park Corner, designs for Lord Shelburne (2A)
36. Piccadilly at Hyde Park Corner, designs for Lord Barrymore (2A)
37. Apsley House, Piccadilly (2A)
38. Deputy Ranger's Lodge, Green Park (2A)
39. 19 Arlington Street (2A)
40. 23 Arlington Street (2A)
41. 19 Dover Street (2A)
42. Carlton House, Pall Mall (2B)
43. 34 Pall Mall (2B)
44. Cumberland House, Pall Mall (2B)
45. Haymarket Opera House (2B)
46. 11 St James's Square (2B)
47. 20 St James's Square (2B)
48. 33 St James's Square (2B)

Introduction

There are few architects who have been the subject of such intense study as Robert Adam (Fig. 1). He was born in Edinburgh in 1728, the second son of the architect William Adam, and was brought up in comfort and wealth at the family estate of Blair Adam near Edinburgh, amid the intellectual environment of the Scottish Enlightenment.[1] According to his obituary, Adam was educated at Edinburgh University among some of the finest minds of his generation, only abandoning his studies in 1745 to join his father's architectural practice, and later assisting his elder brother John, who took control of the firm on the death of their father in 1748.[2] The Adam family's Edinburgh office was a burgeoning one, undertaking lucrative commissions such as Hopetoun House and the Hanoverian Highland Forts.

Fig 1. Attributed to George Willison, *Robert Adam*, *c*.1770–75. NPG 2953. © National Portrait Gallery, London

---

[1] H.M. Colvin, *A biographical dictionary of British architects: 1600-1840*, 2008, p. 44.
[2] Robert Adam's obituary, *The Gentleman's Magazine*, March 1792, pp. 282-83.

Even at this early stage of his career Adam was starting to show signs of exceptional talent and was regarded by his family as something of a prodigy. During his time in the family firm he earned a fortune of around £5,000, which enabled him to undertake a Grand Tour in 1754–8, travelling through France to Italy in order to continue his architectural education and improve his drawing under the tutelage of the French artist Charles-Louis Clérisseau.[3] The drawing style that Adam cultivated in Italy was freer and less contrived than the conventional, old-fashioned manner he had learned in his father's office in Scotland, and under Clérisseau's guidance he developed an elegant sketch-like technique. It was this, combined with a new-found understanding of antique architecture and its decorative motifs that enabled Adam to establish himself as the country's leading neoclassicist after his return to Britain in 1758.

Adam was no wide-eyed tourist. Alongside the educational opportunities that his Grand Tour offered, he also undertook a project which was intended to propel him to celebrity. From Venice, Adam travelled across the Adriatic with a team of draughtsmen to Spalatro in Dalmatia (now Split, Croatia) in order to compile material for an architectural treatise, *The Ruins of the Palace of the Emperor Diocletian at Spalatro in Dalmatia* (1764). Earlier architectural treatises in Britain, such as Robert Wood's *The Ruins of Palmyra* (1753), tended to focus on the public and religious architectural styles of the antique, while Adam's book provided the British public with their first in-depth taste of domestic antique architecture, albeit on a grand scale, in the form of an Imperial palace. Furthermore, the publication helped legitimise Adam's novel ideas for domestic planning and interior decoration.

It is significant that when Adam returned to Britain in 1758 he chose to set up his own architectural practice in Mayfair, London, rather than return to the family practice in his native Edinburgh, as originally planned. When he finally settled at 75 Lower Grosvenor Street, he filled the house with artworks, and carefully arranged pieces from his collection of antiquities (Fig. 2). Gradually he attracted a circle of wealthy patrons, who commissioned from him a diverse array of buildings and interiors. He was joined by his younger brother James in 1763 following his own Grand Tour and together, the Adam brothers built up their architectural office by employing numerous professional draughtsmen but never took pupils.[4] They were dictatorial over design and only allowed schemes to be developed for which they had produced the initial concept, and for which they took ultimate credit. Preliminary sketches were dutifully copied out by the draughtsman as measured and often colour-washed finished drawings which were presented to clients, and working drawings were produced to instruct on-site craftsmen.[5] The drawings were also recopied as office record drawings, resulting in a vast collection.

The Adam office promoted its designs as a deliberate contrast to the more severe Palladian style that had dominated Britain in the preceding decades. The brothers cleverly wielded a cache of neoclassical motifs alongside excitingly varied room shapes: their style was not based on dogmatic archaeological accuracy as the neo-Palladian style had been, but was rather a fusion of all they had seen abroad, merged with what they had learnt of architecture in Britain. With their distinctive, delicate interior decorative style and their bold, rippling architecture,

[3] A.A. Tait, *The Adam Brothers in Rome: Drawings from the Grand Tour*, 2008, pp. 63-65.
[4] A. Rowan, 'The Adam Brothers and Contemporary Office Practice' in G. Worsley (ed.), *Adam in Context: Georgian Group Symposium*, 1992, pp. 42-44.
[5] F. Sands, 'Adam at work', *Country Life*, 2 April 2014, pp. 80-81.

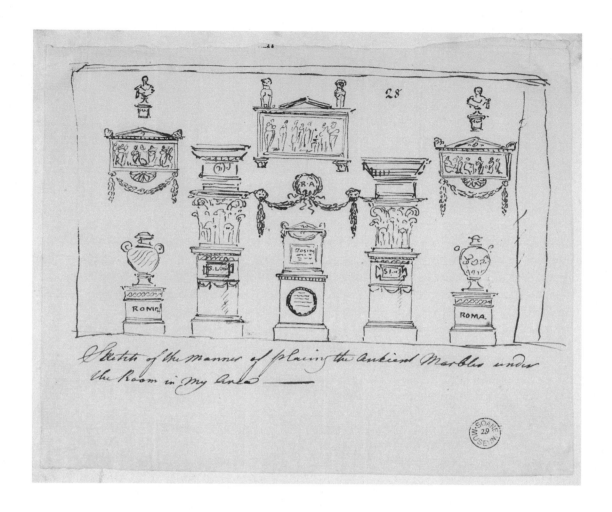

Fig 2. Robert Adam, an arrangement for marbles at 75 Lower Grosvenor Street, 1759. SM Adam volume 54/3/28. Photograph: Ardon Bar-Hama

the Adam brothers became enormously successful. Among their best-known surviving works are those at Kedleston Hall, Derbyshire; Syon House, Brentford; Osterley Park, Hounslow; Culzean Castle, Ayrshire and the Edinburgh Register House. Through such successes the brothers amassed considerable wealth, but it was not to last.

Late in 1767 Robert and James agreed to develop streets of houses on the Marylebone Estate of the Duke of Portland, at what became Portland Place; but soon after, in 1768, they also agreed, in partnership with their brothers John and William, to take a lease of ground on the riverfront near the Strand for another speculative development of houses, known as the Adelphi (see pp. 50, 19). Managing two such vast and expensive projects proved beyond the Adams' reach, especially as they had borrowed heavily in the expectation of securing higher prices for their houses than they were ultimately worth. A crash in their fortunes was undoubtedly coming but was precipitated in 1772 when a run on the Scottish banks triggered a crippling recession. The brothers struggled to sell the Adelphi houses and only escaped bankruptcy by acquiring a private Act of Parliament to sell their properties via a public lottery.[6] The family's finances were stabilised but their debts remained, and thereafter the Adams never managed to replicate their earlier successes, nor did they recover their former reputation. Perhaps unsurprisingly, Robert died aged only 64 in 1792 followed by James in 1794.

The Adam drawings collection

Within ten years of Adam's death in 1792, fashion had changed to such an extent that there was little remaining interest in the surviving designs from his office. On James's death in 1794 the brothers' personal effects and drawings were inherited by their younger brother William and two spinster sisters, Elizabeth and Margaret, who had acted as Robert and James's housekeepers during their decades in London.[7] After James's death in 1794, the remaining siblings were short of money and matters worsened in 1801 when William was declared bankrupt; the Adam company had never fully recovered from its debts following the Adelphi crash, and William continued the contracting business in much the same unrealistic vein as before.[8]

Desperation led William to sell his brothers' possessions at Christie's in 1818 and 1821. Happily, however, many of their works of art and antiquities were purchased by Sir John Soane and are accessible to the public at Sir John Soane's Museum, London (Fig. 3). William's attempts to sell the office drawings began as early as 1802 but interest was lacking: the Adam-style was now obsolete and not yet old enough to attract antiquarian interest. In an attempt to make the drawings saleable, William – with the help of a niece, Susannah Clerk, who had travelled to London in 1810 to care for her elderly relatives – dismantled the original rolls of office drawings which had been arranged by commission, heavily edited the collection and affixed what remained into typologically arranged folios.[9] Unfortunately this process destroyed a large number of the drawings as well as the archaeology of the collection, stripping the identity of patron and place from thousands of designs.

William committed suicide in 1822 and Susannah inherited all he had – the newly bound drawings collection – which she took to Edinburgh following her uncle's death, residing with her bachelor brother Lord Eldin, the famous Scottish judge. She too experienced difficulties in selling the drawings and was even rejected by the British Museum. After several failed attempts to find a buyer, Sir John Soane was approached in 1833. He agreed to take the collection but only for the extraordinarily low price of £200.[10] The drawings were delivered to Soane as deck

---

[6] A. Rowan, *Vaulting Ambition. The Adam Brothers: Contractors to the Metropolis in the Reign of George III*, 2007, pp. 23-24.

[7] A.A. Tait, 'The Sale of Robert Adam's Drawings', *Burlington Magazine*, July 1978, p. 452.

[8] Rowan, 2007, pp. 39-40.

[9] I.G. Brown, 'Robert Adam's drawings: Edinburgh's loss, London's gain', *The Book of the Old Edinburgh Club*, new series 2, 1992, pp. 23-33.

[10] Tait, 1978, p. 454.

Fig 3. Sir Thomas
Lawrence, *Portrait of Sir
John Soane, aged 76,*
1828–29. SM P11.
Photograph: Geremy Butler

cargo on the Soho Steamer as doubtless Susannah was unwilling to pay for more expensive couriering by coach when she had achieved such a low sale price.

Soane left his house-museum as an academy of architecture to the British nation with a private Act of Parliament, and apart from occasional loans to exhibitions and partial war evacuation, the 8,000-strong Adam office drawings collection has not left the Soane Museum since its arrival in 1833. Alongside Soane's collection of 1,000 Adam Grand Tour drawings, these comprise the largest single group of items within the collection at the Soane Museum. They are a much loved and heavily used resource, preserved thanks to Soane's legacy. Adam is remembered as a pioneer of neoclassicism in Britain, who produced designs for more than 350 different patrons. His vast body of work – perhaps best illustrated in the drawings at the Soane Museum – spans the breadth of Britain and has influenced generations. However, there is no place in the world for which Adam made more designs than he did for his adopted home of London.

Robert Adam's London

Adam was based in London from 1758 until his death in 1792. The density of his designs for this one city is extraordinary – especially when we consider that he was never able to secure the big public commissions, which invariably went to his rival, William Chambers. Over 1,700 drawings for Adam designs in London survive at the Soane Museum – almost a quarter of the entire office drawings collection – and these encompass a vast array of building types: domestic terraced houses, urban palaces, public and commercial buildings, speculative projects and commemorative schemes. Moreover, these were produced for a surprisingly wide range of clients, both male and female, including royalty, aristocrats, gentlemen, merchants, institutions and public bodies.

This book reviews a wide variety of the designs Adam made for projects in London, both executed and unexecuted, and it highlights lesser-known buildings as well as familiar ones. Adam's most significant London schemes have received considerable scholarly attention, but here these projects are drawn together as a single corpus of work, using Adam's surviving drawings from the Soane Museum to explore and illustrate the various schemes.

The grandest of Adam's London townhouses, such as 20 St James's Square, 23 Grosvenor Square and 20 Portman Square, are well known, as are his large-scale speculative developments at the Adelphi and Portland Place. However, here we consider not just the surviving beauties of Robert Adam's London but also his aspirations for the city. On Portland Place he had intended to complement the grand brick-and-stucco terraces with several urban palaces on a scale rivalling those of Continental capitals; for Westminster Abbey, he designed funerary monuments; and in the commercial world he made designs for well-known London organisations such as Lloyd's, Lincoln's Inn and the Theatre Royal on Drury Lane.

While the variety of Adam's work in London is greater than most realise, the majority of his focus was on townhouses for the city's burgeoning population. The eighteenth century was one of relative security and prosperity that saw the mercantile and landowning classes acquire London property at an accelerated pace, resulting in a proliferation of urban shopkeepers, artisans and craftspeople to cater to the wealthy. In 1700, London's population was 555,500; by 1801 it had almost doubled to 959,000.[11]

With the exception of churches, occasional aristocratic palaces such as Adam's Lansdowne House and Northumberland House, and a handful of public or commercial buildings such as hospitals and the Inns of Court, the majority of properties in Georgian London were residential, and part of a terrace. This mode of living was a response to overcrowding, as it allowed the maximum number of properties to be squeezed onto a single street frontage and resulted in an abundance of long, narrow building plots.[12] Unlike most other capital cities in Europe, which favoured horizontal apartment-style residences, almost the entire population of London lived vertically in terraced houses of one sort or another. Typically these properties were constructed of London stock brick, perhaps with Portland stone or stucco dressings and with roof timbers and partition walls in cheap imported Baltic fir. Roofs were composed of tiles – until 1765

---

[11]   E. Jones and C. Woodward, *Guide to the architecture of London*, 2013, p. 20.
[12]   J. Summerson, *Georgian London*, 2003, p. 49.

when Lord Penrhyan began to export cheap slate from Wales – and windows were glazed in Crown glass, usually manufactured in Newcastle.[13]

The layout of a terraced property generally followed the same simple formula, with a room at the front and rear on each floor, a staircase, hall or passageway to one side, and often an additional wing to the rear. Despite this apparent lack of variety, room use, ornamentation and decorative schemes were infinitely diverse. For the eighteenth-century elite, a London townhouse was a social or political necessity rather than a luxury, and Adam's ingenuity lay in his ability to improve the townhouse's architectural composition beyond the perceived confines of its restrictive plot. The inclusion of several London townhouses in his retrospective publication the *Works in architecture of Robert and James Adam* (1773–78, 1779) served to bolster the credibility of this genre of architectural activity.

As a master of the terraced house floor plan, Adam excelled in manipulating room uses and varying the positioning of doors and stairwells, and he incorporated apses into his planning to create a series of spaces which achieved a sense of flow and cohesion. As Roy Porter put it, Adam made life in town 'stylish'.[14] The grandest of Adam's townhouses, such as 23 Grosvenor Square and 20 St James's Square, were an elaborate conduit for social parade, giving over the front rooms to the reception of guests and confining the private spaces to a rear wing. However, Adam also provided equally successful interiors in more typical domestic compositions where the public and private rooms were mixed together, as at 33 St James's Square, 34 Pall Mall, and at Mansfield Street and Portland Place.

Furthermore, Adam's abilities as an interior designer were of obvious benefit in town. His townhouse schemes were the perfect vehicle for display at the heart of social activity. A London interior could provide an indicator of the modish innovations out of reach at an owner's country house: the embodiment of their dynastic stability. This was a matter of taste and patronage. Just think of Sir Nathaniel Curzon's rotunda-style saloon at Kedleston Hall; Robert Child's French, English and Italian themed state apartment at Osterley; or the Duke of Northumberland's proto-neo-Gothic chapel at Alnwick Castle. For each of these clients – and many others – Adam provided designs for both country and town. His brilliance with urban interior decoration was an ability to distil the ornamental vigour of a grand country house into the comparatively diminutive spaces of a terraced house.

Given this tradition in London of living in terraces, Adam's clients were often concerned more with the accommodation and interior decoration of their townhouse than they were with its outward appearance.[15] However, there were some notable exceptions, perhaps the most obvious example being Sir Rowland Winn at 11 St James's Square, for which Adam designed a conspicuously fashionable façade to mask an older house behind (see p. 130). For twenty years Sir Rowland was Adam's patron at Nostell Priory, West Yorkshire. He was a man who sought to establish himself in society, often with frustrating results, and he spent a vast sum of money trying to pursue a political career.[16] Sir Rowland almost bankrupted his family through

[13] Ibid., pp. 65-68.
[14] R. Porter, *London: a social history*, 1994, p. 114.
[15] R. Stewart, *The townhouse in Georgian London*, 2009, p. 167.
[16] J.F. Quinn, 'Yorkshiremen go to the Polls: County Contests in the Early Eighteenth Century', *Northern History*, 1985, pp. 137-174.

his architectural and political ambitions. Moreover, the family spent little time in London on account of the Swiss Lady Winn's lack of English language skills.[17] This may explain the unusual arrangement of giving 11 St James's Square a showy Adam frontage, but with minimal interventions inside.

Adam's designs for buildings in London are far too numerous to be explored comprehensively, but in this book you will find a wide selection, including case studies from across the breadth of London's topography and social strata. Each of the projects is plotted on Horwood's map of London (of 1792–99), starting with his early designs on Whitehall and at Westminster Abbey, and then moving roughly around the city in a counter-clockwise direction. It is hoped that this book will enable you to recognise Adam's work as you move around the city, as well as to envisage London as it might have been if more of Adam's ingenious designs had been executed, and if more of those that were had survived demolition.

Whitehall

The famous location of Charles I's execution, Whitehall connects Charing Cross to the north with Westminster to the south. Its foundation is medieval and came about when York Place, the London home of the Archbishops of York, was created. This was confiscated by Henry VIII in 1530 following the fall of Cardinal Wolsey and renamed 'Whitehall Palace' in c.1532 after its white ashlar stone. Initially the name applied only to the northern portion of the street outside the palace, while that to the south – previously very narrow – was known as King Street. This was widened as an extension to Whitehall during the eighteenth and nineteenth centuries and is now largely government offices.[18]

The Admiralty screen

Beside Whitehall Palace was a carpenters' yard and in 1572 this was leased by the Crown for the construction of Wallingford House by Sir Francis Knollys. In 1622 Wallingford House was purchased for £3,000 from the Knollys family by George Villiers, 1st Duke of Buckingham, the Lord High Admiral, and became the headquarters of the Royal Navy until the foundation of the Ministry of Defence in 1964. Wallingford House was demolished following a fire in 1694 and was replaced by the first purpose-built Admiralty building, erected by a carpenter, John Evans.[19] However, with time this proved inadequate, and once the Admiralty had acquired the freehold in 1720, Evans's building was replaced in 1723–36 to designs by Thomas Ripley.[20]

Ripley's Admiralty was built in brick with stone dressings, repeating the U-shaped plan and pediment of the preceding structure. To enable the widening of Whitehall, in 1759 the Lords of the Admiralty agreed to sell a portion of Ripley's forecourt for £650 to the Westminster Bridge

[17] C. Todd, 'A Swiss Milady in Yorkshire: Sabine Winn of Nostell Priory', *Yorkshire Archaeological Journal 77*, 2005, pp. 205-224.
[18] B. Weinreb, C. Hibbert, J. Keay and J. Keay, *The London Encyclopaedia*, 2008, pp. 1019-20.
[19] *Survey of London* (hereafter SoL), Volume XVI, 1935, p. 45.
[20] Colvin, 2008, p. 870.

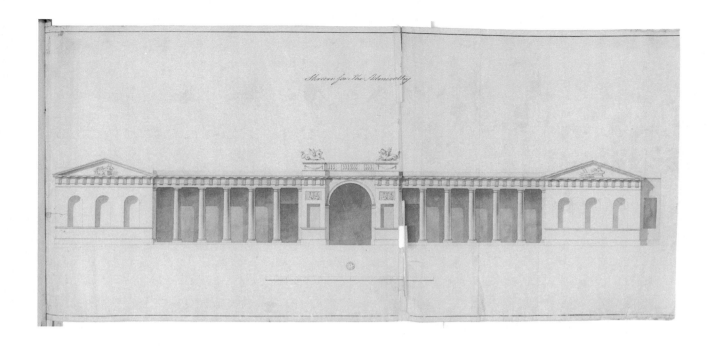

Fig 4. Adam office, design for the Admiralty screen, 1759. SM Adam volume 35/1. Photograph: Ardon Bar-Hama

Commissioners; Ripley's boundary wall was demolished and a new wall commissioned.[21] Only recently returned from his Grand Tour, Adam is thought to have received the commission for the new wall thanks to the influence of two Lords of the Admiralty: his neighbour from Kinross-shire, Sir Gilbert Elliott of Minto, and the Hon. Edward Boscawen, for whose wife – the Bluestocking Fanny Boscawen – he was decorating their residence at Hatchlands, Surrey.

There are six Adam drawings for the Admiralty screen at the Soane Museum (Fig. 4).[22] These show a triumphal arch (loosely based on the Arch of Titus, Rome), flanked by Doric colonnaded links, and pedimented lodges containing niches. The whole is decorated with nautical ornaments including the prows of ships and marine creatures, all carved by Michael Henry Spang.[23] The relief panels to either side of the arch, depicting boys holding dolphin tails, were repeated by Adam in the centre of the drawing room ceiling at Hatchlands for the Boscawens. Figurative sculptures are included in an Adam office perspective showing the screen in the context of a bustling Whitehall, by the draughtsman Agostino Brunias (Fig. 5), but it is unlikely that these were executed, as they do not appear in any other contemporary views. The design was extremely innovative, being an early example of Adam's architectural 'movement', with the columns casting dramatic shadows

[21] SoL, Volume XVI, 1935, pp. 58-59.
[22] All drawings from Sir John Soane's collection can be consulted at Soane Collections Online: http://collections.soane.org/home?_ga=1.230365020.159961063.1449759424
[23] I. Roscoe, *A biographical dictionary of sculptors in Britain: 1600-1851*, 2009, pp. 1161-62.

Fig 5. Adam office, view of Whitehall including the Admiralty screen, 1759. SM Adam volume 35/4. Photograph: Ardon Bar-Hama

against the blank wall behind. Its striking appearance is most successful in drawing the eye away from Ripley's ungainly Admiralty building beyond.

Adam was clearly very proud of the Admiralty screen, built in 1760–61, which is not surprising given its sophisticated modernity and the fact that it was his first public building and first London commission. He had Brunias's perspective engraved by Francis Patton, and the published engraving was sold from February 1761, along with another by Patton showing Adam's own plan and elevation of the screen, at Andrew Millar's bookshop on the Strand for 2s 6d.[24] Moreover, Adam included a second engraved version of the perspective (by Domenico Cunego) in the first volume of the *Works in architecture...* (the plan and elevation were later reproduced in the posthumous third volume, in 1822).[25]

[24]   A.T. Bolton, *The architecture of Robert and James Adam*, 1922, Volume II, Index p. 34.
[25]   Adam, Volume I, 1773-78, part iv, pl. 1; Volume III, 1822, pl. 12.

Fig 6. The Admiralty Screen, Whitehall, 2014. Photograph: Daniela Stallinger

Two large openings were formed in the screen in 1827–28 to designs by George Ledwell Taylor in order to allow access for the Duke of Clarence's carriage. Happily, however, this damage was reversed in 1923 and the screen survives as it was executed in accordance with Adam's design (Fig. 6).

Westminster Abbey – *funerary monuments*

One of the most under-studied elements of Adam's work is his production of funerary monuments and mausolea. In London, he was responsible for designing seven monuments for Westminster Abbey.

Westminster Abbey is two hundred yards south of St James's Park. Its early history is unclear, although the first Royal burial here was that of Harold I in 1040. The Abbey was rebuilt by Edward the Confessor and consecrated in 1065. Following Edward's canonisation in 1139, generations of royal patronage was stimulated in devotion to his cult, the greatest example being the second rebuilding of the Abbey from 1245 by Henry III. These works continued for centuries, only for the monastery to be disbanded at the Dissolution. However, the Abbey itself was saved and transformed into the Cathedral of Westminster. During the Civil War, Cromwell's troops famously camped inside the Abbey, causing considerable damage and resulting in a programme of restoration works in 1698–1723, to designs by Sir Christopher Wren.[26]

Doubtless prompted by the burials of Edward the Confessor and Henry III, the Abbey became a popular mausoleum, and by the eighteenth century was becoming crowded. During the course of his career, Adam's designs for Westminster Abbey ranged from monuments to William Dalrymple, an eighteen-year-old midshipman killed in a clash with the French off the coast of Virginia, to Elizabeth Percy, 1st Duchess of Northumberland; and from Mary Hope, the wife of a prosperous merchant, to the famous poet James Thomson.[27] Of seven monuments, only one – Adam's first design for the Abbey – a monument to Major-General James Wolfe of 1759, was not executed (Fig. 7). In addition, Adam himself is buried in the south transept beside his great rival Sir William Chambers. Joseph Nollekens designed a monument for Adam which was not executed,[28] and instead there is a simple wall tablet inscribed: *ROBERT ADAM Esquire / ARCHITECT / born at Kirkaldie / 3rd July 1728 / died in London / 3rd March 1792.*

It is interesting to compare Adam's unexecuted scheme for Wolfe with that for his military colleague, Lieutenant-Colonel Roger Townshend, whose monument was designed for the Abbey by Adam only months later in 1760 (Fig. 8). James Wolfe was the eldest son of Lieutenant-General Edward Wolfe, while Roger Townshend was the fifth son of the 3rd Viscount Townshend (of Raynham Hall, Norfolk, later Adam's patron). Wolfe commanded the British forces in Canada and died in battle from three gunshot wounds five days before the surrender of Quebec. He was hailed a national hero who had given his life for a triumphal victory and his monument was publicly funded.[29] Townshend, who served in America, died when he was hit by a cannon-ball at Ticonderoga fighting the French, and his monument was a personal tribute from his mother.[30]

---

[26] S. Bradley and N. Pevsner, *The buildings of England: London 6: Westminster*, 2003, p. 110.
[27] F. Sands, 'Robert Adam: a designer of mausolea and monuments', *Mausolus*, Winter 2014, pp. 5-7.
[28] Roscoe, 2009, p. 911.
[29] *Oxford Dictionary of National Biography* online (hereafter ODNB): James Wolfe: http://www.oxforddnb.com/view/article/29833?docPos=1 (accessed 3/08/2016).
[30] G. Beard, *The work of Robert Adam*, 1978, p. 55.

Fig 7. Adam office, design for a funerary monument to Major-General James Wolfe for Westminster Abbey, 1759. SM Adam volume 28/50. Photograph: Ardon Bar-Hama

As a public commission, the Wolfe monument design was the subject of a competition and other schemes were submitted by Sir William Chambers and Joseph Wilton.[31] Adam was surely lured by the fame that a public commission of this calibre would afford and he made six variant designs for the monument: the final scheme features a sarcophagus containing an inscription panel, flanked by columns ornamented with military trophies, and surmounted by a relief panel showing Wolfe's death scene, which in turn is flanked by antique military figures, and surmounted by military trophies attended by the figures of Victory and two defeated enemies, and the whole is set against a pyramid in relief. Adam's design was rejected in favour of one

---

[31] D. King, *The complete works of Robert and James Adam and unbuilt Adam*, 2001, Volume II, p. 261.

Fig 8. Adam office, design for a funerary monument to
Lieutenant-Colonel Roger Townshend for Westminster
Abbey, 1760. SM Adam volume 19/10. Photograph: Ardon
Bar-Hama

by Wilton, but the composition
was not entirely abandoned as
elements of it reappeared a few
months later in his designs for
the Townshend monument.

The Townshend monument
is composed of two atlantes
(male caryatids), flanking an
inscription panel and supporting
a sarcophagus containing a death-
scene relief panel, surmounted by
military trophies, and set against
a pyramid in relief. In Adam's
drawing the atlantes are shown as
antique slaves, but in execution
they were Native American
warriors, presumably referring
to the location of Townshend's
death. They establish a pleasing
stylistic contrast with the rest
of the monument, which is
entirely classical. It has been
noted by John Fleming that the
composition of a sarcophagus
supported by figures may
have been inspired by Italian
Renaissance monuments such
as that for Pietro Lombardo at
SS. Giovanni e Paolo, Venice.[32]
But it should be added that
Adam owned a drawing by
his tutor Clérisseau of Roman
tombs, among them two tombs
comprising strigilated caskets
supported by terms that are
reminiscent of the Townshend
design, suggesting that Adam's
sources may have been more
varied.[33]

---

[32] J. Fleming, 'Robert Adam, Luc-François Breton and the Townshend monument in Westminster Abbey',
Connoisseur, April 1962, p. 169.
[33] SM Adam volume 57/20.

The most notable similarity between the Wolfe and Townshend monument designs is the central death-scene relief panel. In both, the protagonist is shown reclining, surrounded by comrades, with the battle continuing in the background. It is not known if Viscountess Townshend was familiar with Adam's design for the Wolfe monument, but it is likely given that its death scene features another of her sons, George Townshend, to whom Wolfe is gesturing as his second-in-command. The Townshend monument is signed by Benjamin Carter but it is generally agreed that Joseph Eckstein, who signed the marble death-scene relief panel, was responsible for much of the work. A terracotta model for the panel was made in Rome by Luc-François Breton.[34] The Townshend monument remains *in situ* in the south aisle of Westminster Abbey, although some of the heads of the figures in the death-scene relief have been lost.

Timeline of Adam's designs for monuments at Westminster Abbey:

1759: Public commission for a monument to Major-General James Wolfe (d.1759), unexecuted.

1760: Viscountess Townshend commissions Adam to design a monument to her son, Lieutenant-Colonel Roger Townshend (d.1759), executed by Benjamin Carter and Joseph Eckstein in the south aisle.

1762: Andrew Millar (bookseller) and Patrick Murdock (writer) commission Adam to design a monument to James Thomson (poet, d.1748), executed by Michael Henry Spang in the south transept.

c.1767: John Hope (merchant) commissions Adam to design a monument to his wife Mary (d.1767), executed by unknown sculptor in the south transept.

1778: 1st Duke of Northumberland commissions Adam to design a monument to his wife the Duchess (d.1776), executed by Nicholas Reed in the Chapel of St Nicholas.

c.1780–82: George III commissions Adam to design a monument to Major John André (d.1780), executed by Peter Mathias Van Gelder in the south aisle.

c.1782–83: Sir John Dalrymple, 4th Baronet commissions Adam to design a monument to his son, Midshipman William Dalrymple (d.1782), executed by an unknown sculptor in the south aisle.

Northumberland House, Strand

Northumberland House, at the western end of the Strand, was built *c.*1605–12 by Henry Howard, Earl of Northampton to designs by Bernard Jansen.[35] It was one of London's finest

---

[34] Fleming, 1962, pp. 164-70.
[35] Colvin, 2008, p. 569.

Jacobean mansions. On Northampton's death in 1614, the house passed to his nephew, Thomas Howard, 1st Earl of Suffolk, whose son, the 2nd Earl, included it as part of his daughter Elizabeth's settlement when she married Algernon Percy, 10th Earl of Northumberland in 1642. The house remained with the Percy family – coming to be known as Northumberland House – until its sale to the Metropolitan Board of Works in 1874 for £500,000, following which it was demolished for the creation of Northumberland Avenue.[36] Numerous programmes of alterations were carried out during its history, and it was during the tenure of the 1st Duke and Duchess of Northumberland that Adam was commissioned to make designs for the interior.

Hugh Smithson succeeded his father, Sir Langdale Smithson, as 4th Baronet in 1727, aged seventeen, and went on to inherit estates and wealth from his sister and cousin. The Smithson family had made a fortune in haberdashery on Cheapside and bought the Stanwick estate near Catterick in 1638. The 1st Baronet had been created by Charles II in 1663, having supported Charles I during the Civil War. In 1740 Sir Hugh married Lady Elizabeth Percy, the daughter of the 7th Duke of Somerset and a grand-daughter of the 11th Earl of Northumberland. As Elizabeth's only sibling, George, had died of smallpox during his Grand Tour in 1744, she inherited everything in 1750 from both the Dukedom of Somerset and the Earldom of Northumberland. This brought Sir Hugh not only the estates of Syon and Alnwick Castle, but also Northumberland House, and the Earldom, elevating him – through a special arrangement with George II – to the title of 12th Earl of Northumberland.[37]

In 1766 the Earl was created 1st Duke of Northumberland (of the third creation). His incredible rise was partly thanks to his marriage, partly thanks to a friendship with Lord Bute (his son married Bute's daughter in 1764) and partly thanks to his various public offices. He had served as MP for Middlesex from 1740 until 1750, when his elevation to the Earldom took him into the House of Lords, where he became an active member. He was also Sheriff of Yorkshire in 1738–39; Trustee of the British Museum in 1753-86; Lord of the Bedchamber in 1753–63; Lord Lieutenant of Northumberland in 1753–86; Lord Lieutenant of Middlesex in 1762–86; Vice-Admiral of North America in 1764 and Master of the Horse in 1778–80. Moreover, he was a skilled land manager, exploiting coal reserves and increasing the financial yields of his estates, enabling him to undertake rebuilding works across the country.[38] By these means, Northumberland became a great patron of the arts and his Duchess was a renowned connoisseur.[39]

Adam started his work for Northumberland at Syon in 1761, and at Alnwick Castle in 1769. In 1770 he took over from James Paine to decorate the interiors at Northumberland House.[40] His work there comprised schemes for two reception rooms: the dining room and drawing room, both at the rear of the house overlooking the garden. Twenty-four Adam office drawings for this work survive at the Soane Museum. One of these is Adam's 1770 design for a ceiling for

[36] SoL, Volume XVIII, 1937, chapter 2.
[37] ODNB: 1st Duke of Northumberland: http://www.oxforddnb.com/view/article/21943?docPos=6 (accessed 11/08/2016).
[38] Ibid.
[39] ODNB: Elizabeth Percy, Duchess of Northumberland: http://www.oxforddnb.com/view/article/59609?docPos=2 (accessed 11/08/2016).
[40] Colvin, 2008, pp. 49, 769.

Fig 9. Adam office, design for the chimney wall for the glass drawing room at Northumberland House, 1770–73. SM Adam volume 39/6. Photograph: Ardon Bar-Hama

the dining room, but this is not thought to have been executed. More significant are Adam's designs for the renowned glass drawing room.

The glass drawing room won fame on account of its being lined with painted glass, which was further ornamented with gilt metalwork and mirrors integrated into the glazed wall surface. The surviving drawings for the scheme show the walls in dotted red to represent porphyry, while the pilasters, dado and frieze are green (Fig. 9). The ceiling design has a central medallion enclosed within an octagon with four radiating arms connecting to lunettes, and was inspired by the Udine Peruzzi loggia at the Villa Madama in Rome.[41] It was one of the most colourful Adam ceilings in London and the drawing for its design is one of the most beautiful Adam drawings in the world (Fig. 10).

The glass drawing room was altered in 1818–24 when the south front of the house was found to be structurally unsound and rebuilt to designs by Thomas Cundy necessitating the widening of the room. The wall panels were modified and a cove was added to Adam's ceiling.[42] Unfortunately, the ceiling was then destroyed on the demolition of the house in 1874, while the glass on the walls was dismantled and removed in crates to the riding school at Syon.[43] In 1945

[41] E. Harris, *The genius of Robert Adam: his interiors,* 2001, p. 100.
[42] Ibid., p. 103.
[43] D. Stillman, *The decorative work of Robert Adam*, 1966, p. 102.

Fig 10. Adam office, design for the ceiling for the glass drawing room at Northumberland House, 1770. SM Adam volume 11/33. Photograph: Geremy Butler

these panels were sold to Bert Crowther of Syon Lodge, who leased them as temporary décor for parties, and in 1953 the remains of the room were purchased by the Victoria and Albert Museum and a small part is now on display in the British galleries alongside a model of the complete room.[44]

The destruction of the glass drawing room at Northumberland House is a sad loss from Adam's London, not least because the wall treatment was unique in his work. With the exception of the glazed pilasters in the auditorium of David Garrick's Theatre Royal on Drury Lane, Adam did not repeat the heavy use of glass in any other of his interiors. This is perhaps because the room never received the public adulation which Adam may have anticipated; indeed, it was little seen, as soon after its completion in 1775 the Duchess's declining health prevented the couple from entertaining, and her death a year later was a severe blow to her husband.[45]

[44] Beard, 1978, p. 64.
[45] Harris, 2001, p. 99.

The Adelphi

Being keen to raise a building in London on a public scale, Robert Adam and his three brothers in 1768 undertook this vast speculative project to build a complex of roads, townhouses, cottages, shops, a tavern, warehouses, stables and a subterranean roadway. Construction was managed directly by the brothers' own London firm of builders' providers and merchants – William Adam & Co., formed in 1764 – in which they were equal partners. Robert and James were the creative driving force, and would have supplied the architectural designs; John offered structural advice and all-important financial support; William, a trained banker, was in charge of running the company and overseeing the accounts.

The ground in question was Durham Yard, which the brothers agreed to take on a a 99-year lease at £1,200 per annum from the Trustees of the 3rd Duke of St Albans. St Albans himself had fled the country to avoid his creditors.[46] The site was bordered by the River Thames to the south and the Strand to the north and was located between the modern landmarks of Waterloo Bridge and Charing Cross Station. It had taken its name from Durham House, the home of Richard le Poor, a thirteenth-century Bishop of Durham who built the first structure there. Durham House was not demolished until 1660 and after that, until the Adam brothers' intervention, the site was used generally for low-quality housing and light industry.[47]

Without the benefit of any embankment, the plot rose in a muddy slope from the river to the Strand some forty feet above. In 1771, and after lengthy wrangling with the City of London, William Adam & Co. acquired a private Act of Parliament giving them the right to embank the riverside, which they had already begun to do. This was a vital element of the scheme, as it would prevent flooding at high tide and foul odours at low tide. Employing at least 2,000 men, the brothers first cleared the site of all preceding buildings, and, inspired by Robert Adam's experience of Diocletian's Palace on the seafront at Split, they constructed a sequence of vaulted arches in order to raise the development to the level of the Strand (Fig. 11). These arches contained

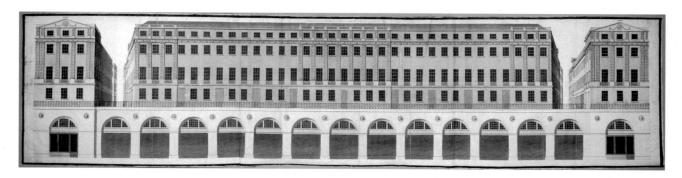

Fig 11. Adam office, design for the Royal Terrace and arches at the Adelphi, *c.*1768–69. SM Adam volume 32/10. Photograph: Geremy Butler

[46] Rowan, 2007, p. 14.
[47] D.G.C. Allan, *The Adelphi: past and present*, 2001, p. 12.

a network of stables, warehouses and subterranean roads.[48] The brothers had counted on leasing the warehouses lucratively, but this did not happen, contributing to the scheme's eventual failure.

The early designs for the layout of the Adelphi can be seen in plans in the King's Topographical Collection at the British Library and London Metropolitan Archives.[49] Including 69 townhouses, the plan cleverly crammed many varied properties on to this relatively small site, maximising the potential profit. The Adelphi also served to memorialise the brothers themselves, with streets named after each one. The early plans do not show the complex exactly as built. The principal differences are seen in John Street, where the Royal Society of Arts took up residence, and on the other side of the development there is a large gap in the houses which was required on the north side opposite Robert Street to allow light to reach the back of James and Thomas Coutts's bank on the Strand – something to which they were legally entitled.[50]

Most of the Adelphi was composed of terraced houses with brick façades, enlivened by pilasters and other dressings of stucco, and metal balconies – made by the Carron Company of Falkirk, in which John was a partner – and bearing Robert Adam's favourite anthemion motif. The properties were technologically advanced. They had plumbed water and there was a water tower – fitted with a lightning conductor – which was fed by the river and gave provision for three fire engines.[51] The largest and most opulent houses were the eleven in the so-called 'Royal Terrace', along the southern boundary of the complex facing the river, with smaller houses on the surrounding streets, a tavern and shops towards the Strand, as well as cottages for less wealthy occupants below the road in front of the Royal Terrace.

As the fabric of the complex was the responsibility of William Adam & Co., the drawings for the engineering and building work would have been the property of that office. However, drawn promotional material and interior decoration were the responsibility of Robert and James Adam's architectural office, so there are 168 drawings for these elements at the Soane Museum. The surviving drawings tell us how Adam amassed the hundreds of designs needed to decorate each and every building. Although it was normally rare for him to reuse designs, this was more common in his speculative work. Many of the designs for chimneypieces for the Adelphi were either duplicates or close variants of other Adam chimneypieces from throughout the 1760s.[52] Inscriptions in Robert's own hand on chimneypiece designs for earlier projects show that he had simply sifted through his work and allocated designs to the various properties on the Adelphi.

Surviving drawings for the Adelphi are mostly for ceilings and chimneypieces. As expected of a speculative development, the ceilings are bright and alluring, in the characteristic Adam-style, and inlaid with elegant painted panels. A particularly fine set of drawings were produced as promotional material showing the Shakespearean actor David Garrick's house at 5 Royal Terrace (Fig. 12). On 1 June 1771 Garrick acquired the lease of his three-bay, four-storey house which was set over a double basement. He was in residence by April 1772, but he had agreed immediately on signing the lease 10 months earlier that his friends the Adam brothers could

---

[48] Ibid., pp. 34-35.
[49] Rowan, 2007, pp. 48-49.
[50] Allan, 2001, p. 40.
[51] Ibid.
[52] I am grateful to Brigid von Preussen, PhD candidate at Columbia University for sharing her research on the provenance of the Adelphi chimneypiece designs.

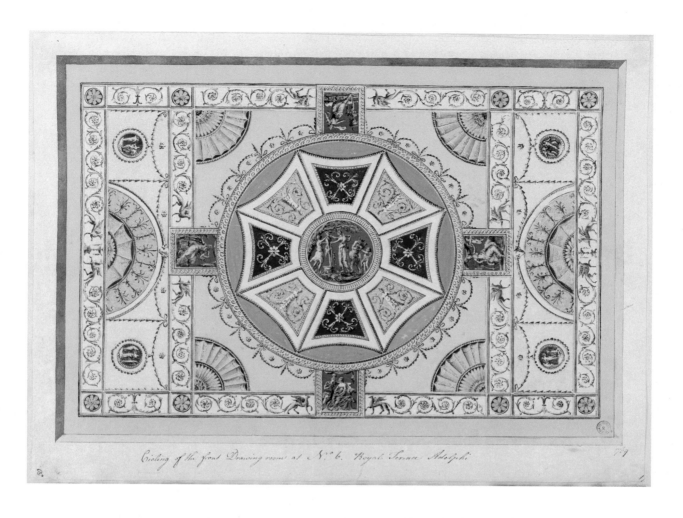

Cieling of the front Drawing room at N.º 6. Royal Terrace Adelphi

Fig 12. Adam office, promotional drawing showing the ceiling for David Garrick's front drawing room at 5 Royal Terrace, Adelphi, 1769. SM Adam volume 13/30. Photograph: Ardon Bar-Hama

use his name to advertise the Adelphi in *Town and Country Magazine*.[53] Three years later Robert and James became Garrick's neighbours when they moved into No. 4.

In 1772 the Adelphi was nearing completion and the brothers were anticipating considerable profits. But they were over-stretched financially, and a run on the Scottish banks, precipitated by the bankruptcy of Neale, James, Fordyce & Downe's bank, caused considerable financial difficulty for the Adam brothers, who had taken out sizeable loans to build the development. They nearly went bankrupt, necessitating John to mortgage the family estate of Blair Adam for

---

[53] *Alan G. Thomas* sale catalogue number 18, 1967.

£36,000, and then in July 1773 (thanks to Robert's position as MP for Kinross), the brothers obtained a private Act of Parliament to sell the Adelphi properties by a lottery and thereby stabilise their finances. The lottery raised £218,500, comprising 4,370 tickets costing £50 each, with 108 prizes of unsold properties and a handful of the Adams' collection of artworks and antiquities. Unsold tickets reverted to William Adam & Co., and when the winning tickets were drawn on 3 March 1774, the brothers were fortunate to receive several prizes themselves, thereby retaining some of the Adelphi property and their art collection. However, even after the lottery, the brothers' debts remained high, and eventually, after John, Robert and James had all died, William was declared bankrupt in 1801.[54]

The lease of the Adelphi site came to an end in 1867 and the property reverted to Messrs Drummonds, who had succeeded to the estates of the Duke of St Albans. Drummonds allowed the renewal of the lease but simultaneously sanctioned numerous alterations including cement rendering and the removal of the metal balconies in 1872.[55] On 2 April and 7 May 1936 auctions were held at Nos 6 and 7 Royal Terrace for the sale of fittings stripped from the Adelphi houses, including chimneypieces, grates, wainscoting, doors, dado rails, columns and balconettes.[56] Then the entire central block was demolished and a new building erected on the site (by then known as the Adelphi Terrace) to designs by Collcutt and Hamp. Other parts of the Adams' complex were demolished piecemeal and all that survives of the Adelphi today are 1-3 Robert Street (much altered internally and with a dormer storey added in 1908); the façades of 6-10 Adam Street (also with a new dormer storey, and with little of the eighteenth-century fabric behind); and the Royal Society of Arts building at 2–8 John Street and 18 Adam Street (which has also received a dormer storey and some internal alterations). It is depressing to think that in the same decade, London lost both Sir John Soane's Bank of England and the Adam brothers' Adelphi.

Theatre Royal, Drury Lane

Running north-west from Aldwych, Drury Lane is an ancient thoroughfare which was called 'old' as early as 1199.[57] The Theatre Royal plot between Drury Lane and Catherine Street has been the location of a theatre longer than any other in London. The original theatre – known as the Theatre Royal on Brydges Street – was built in 1662–63 to designs by an unknown architect for Thomas Killgrew and the King's Company. It was destroyed by fire in 1672 and rebuilt over the next two years to designs by Sir Christopher Wren.[58] It re-opened as the Theatre Royal on Drury Lane, thus establishing the name which survives to this day.[59]

The Theatre won its greatest acclaim during the tenure of David Garrick as manager. Garrick, the son of an impoverished army officer, left the family home in Lichfield in 1737 and walked to London with the intention of studying law.[60] His legal studies at Lincoln's Inn lasted only a few

[54] Rowan, 2007, pp. 23-39.
[55] Weinreb, 2008, p. 7.
[56] Farebrother, Ellis & Co. sale catalogue, *The Adelphi*, 2 April 1936.
[57] Bradley, 2003, p. 345.
[58] SoL, Volume XXXV, 1970, p. 9.
[59] R. Carter, 'The Drury Lane Theatres of Henry Holland and Benjamin Dean Wyatt', *Journal of the Society of Architectural Historians*, October 1967, p. 200.
[60] I. McIntyre, *Garrick*, 1999, p. 27.

days and instead he joined his brother Peter as a vintner with cellars in Durham Yard off the Strand.[61] Despite being a largely unsuccessful venture, it was through this profession that Garrick became acquainted with various theatre managers and in 1740 began working as an amateur playwright and actor, acting professionally from 1741. His first plaudits came playing Richard III at Goodman's Fields Theatre on 19 October 1741.[62] His abilities as an actor propelled him to celebrity. He was credited with an ability to imbue characters with unprecedented naturalism, becoming particularly popular as a tragedian specialising in Shakespearean characters.

In 1747 Garrick invested £12,000 in a half-share of the patent of the Theatre Royal on Drury Lane in partnership with James Lacy, whereby Lacy would manage the property and Garrick the stage. This arrangement endured until Lacy's death in 1774 and made Garrick a wealthy man.[63] He contracted over 300 actors and developed the Theatre into the most popular in London. On his retirement in 1776, Garrick sold his half-share of the Theatre's lease for £35,000 to Dr James Ford, Thomas Linley and Richard Brinsley Sheridan.[64]

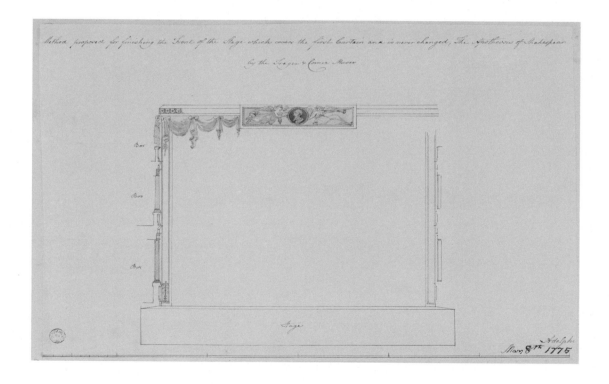

Fig 13. Adam office, design for the proscenium arch at the Drury Lane Theatre, 1775. SM Adam volume 27/85. Photograph: Ardon Bar-Hama

[61] ODNB: David Garrick: http://www.oxforddnb.com/view/article/10408?docPos=1 (accessed 07/01/2016).
[62] J. Benedetti, *David Garrick and the Birth of Modern Theatre*, 2001, p. 47.
[63] McIntyre, 1999, pp. 132-33.
[64] SoL, Volume XXXV, 1970, p. 16

In 1775, just a year before his retirement, Garrick commissioned Adam to Georgianise the Theatre, giving it a new façade and interior. Adam's designs for the proscenium arch and two alternative schemes for the ceiling of the auditorium survive at the Soane Museum. The proscenium arch design is ornamented with a cameo of Shakespeare, but it is not known if it was executed (Fig. 13). Adam's executed 1775 scheme for the ceiling shows a coffered dome and oval oculus, and was achieved in *trompe l'oeil*, but a later design of 1776 shows a compartmental ceiling for the same space suggesting an intention to repaint although this was never done.

Although Adam's work at the Theatre was dictated by the pre-existing fabric, he was certainly proud of the scheme, including both the design for the façade and the executed interior in the *Works in architecture....*[65] As Adam's work at the Theatre has since been lost, these plates

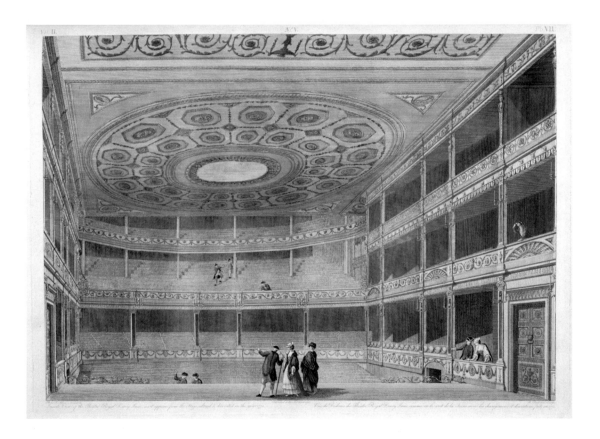

Fig 14. Robert and James Adam, *Works in architecture of Robert and James Adam*, Volume II, 1779, part V, plate 7: view of the interior of the Drury Lane Theatre. Photograph: Geremy Butler

[65]   Adam, Volume II, 1779, part V, plates vi-vii.

comprise the best view of it, with his *trompe l'oeil* ceiling and his treatment of the auditorium seating, ornamented with pilasters faced in coloured glass (Fig. 14). His light-coloured and apparently spacious interior was innovative, with slender columns supporting the balconies, a raised ceiling and a shorter forestage, and it set the pattern for British theatre design for some time to come. In 1783 the interior of the auditorium was redecorated by Thomas Greenwood and William Capon but in 1791 the fabric was declared unsafe and over the next four years it was rebuilt for Sheridan to designs by Henry Holland, only to be destroyed by fire in 1809 and rebuilt again in 1811–12 to designs by Benjamin Dean Wyatt. Wyatt's interior was remodelled in 1822 to designs by Samuel Beazley and again in 1921–22 to designs by J. Embin Walker, F. Edward Jones and Robert Cromie.[66]

Charing Cross

Now a busy junction between the Strand, Northumberland Avenue, Whitehall, The Mall and Cockspur Street, Charing Cross is named after a small hamlet on this site, where Edward I had the last of twelve crosses erected in 1290 to mark the resting places of his wife, Eleanor of Castile's funeral cortège on its journey to Westminster Abbey. Eleanor's Caen stone cross stood in the current location of the statue of Charles I and was only removed in 1647 when the stone was reused. In 1863 a replica of the cross was created and is now in the forecourt of Charing Cross Station.[67]

Drummond's Bank, Charing Cross

Drummond's Bank was founded in 1717 by a goldsmith named Andrew Drummond at the Golden Eagle in Charing Cross. Drummond was descended from the family of the Viscounts Strathallan who had lost their fortune and ventured into trade.[68] The bank became popular, particularly among wealthy Scots – including Adam – and it moved into its own premises at No. 49 on the southern side of Charing Cross in 1760. The origins of this building are unknown.[69]

In 1777 Adam was commissioned to make alterations to the Drummond's building, and from five surviving drawings at the Soane Museum we can see a proposal to rebuild the façade and front commercial rooms, including a subterranean strong room, an apsidal shop and domestic rooms above (Figs 15-16). Adam's elevation shows a three-storey, five-bay building, its central three bays projecting and pedimented, with a central door surmounted by a fanlight and flanked by arched windows and side doors within apses. The design is particularly ornamental for a commercial building, with ornate ironwork balconettes to the first-floor windows, and a sculptural tablet spanning the central three bays between the first- and second-floor windows.

Adam's alterations were partially executed, but the extent of this work and its adherence to the surviving drawings is difficult to gauge, although presumably it was only internal, as Adam's design for the façade does not appear in contemporary views.[70] The Bank was rebuilt

[66] Weinreb, 2008, p. 915.
[67] Ibid., p. 148.
[68] Bolton, 1922, Volume II, Index p. 69.
[69] King, 2001, Volume 2, p. 52.
[70] Ibid.

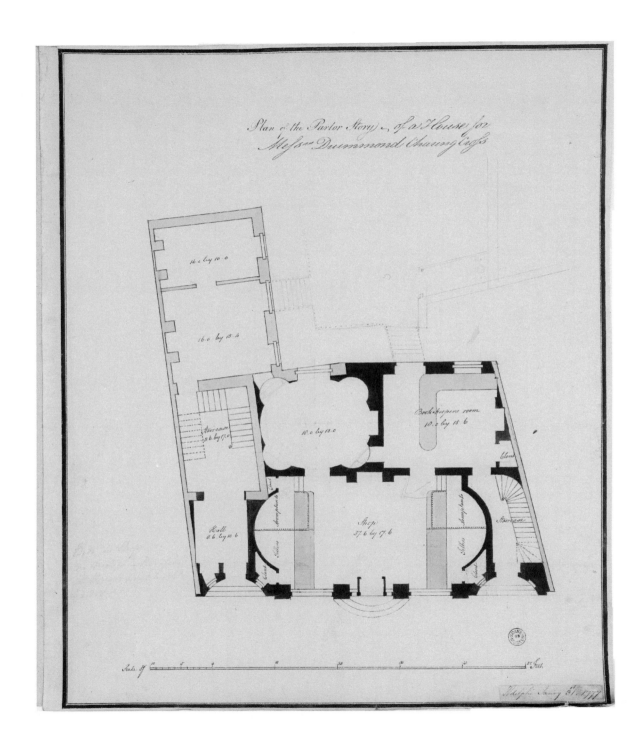

Fig 15. Adam office, plan for alterations to Drummond's Bank, 1777. SM Adam volume 31/118. Photograph: Ardon Bar-Hama

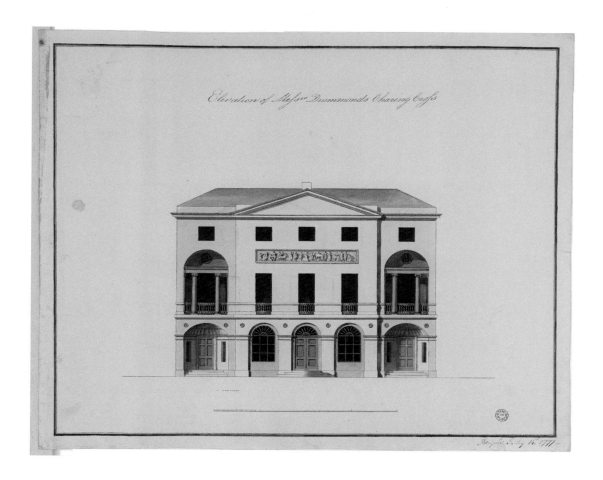

Fig 16. Adam office, design for the façade of Drummond's Bank, 1777. SM Adam volume 31/116.
Photograph: Ardon Bar-Hama

in 1879–81 to designs by P.C. Hardwick, although one Adam chimneypiece from the previous building still survives in the board room.[71] Drummond's Bank merged with the Royal Bank of Scotland in 1924 and the Charing Cross building remains the RBS Drummond's Branch.[72]

King's Bench Prison, Southwark

Taking its name from the law court known as King's Bench, the King's Bench Prison was originally located in Borough High Street, Southwark and dated from the thirteenth or

---

[71] Bradley, 2003, p. 375.
[72] Weinreb, 2008, p. 249.

fourteenth century.[73] It was a public institution built with public money but managed and run under contract for private profit, and was most regularly used as a debtors' prison. It was not until 1752 that the old prison buildings were found to be unfit and were replaced at the expense of the Board of Works, half a mile away on a 2 ½ acre site on Bench Walk (now McCoid Way) near St George's Fields. Completed in 1758, this was larger than many contemporary prisons but was built to a poor standard and quickly became dirty, overcrowded and lacking in adequate security.[74]

The prison was designed to house a maximum of 80 inmates, but owing to the increasing numbers of debtors being sentenced it was holding as many as 413 inmates by 1769. As a consequence, the Prison Marshal petitioned the House of Commons for the institution to be enlarged and enclosed.[75] Adam submitted designs for three alternative improvement schemes

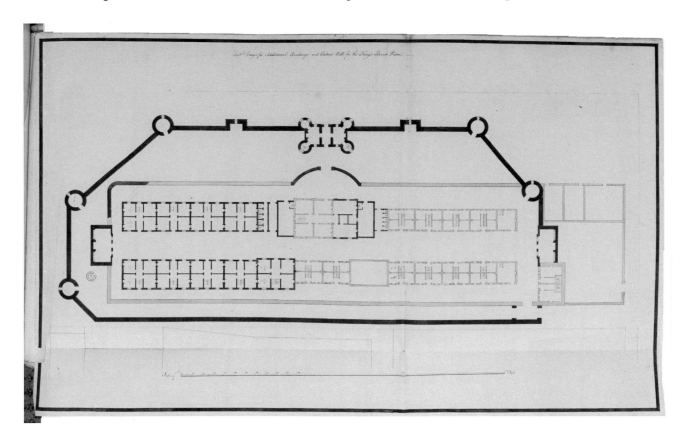

Fig 17. Adam office, plan for the first proposal to extend and enclose King's Bench Prison, 1773. SM Adam volume 38/22. Photograph: Ardon Bar-Hama

[73] SoL, Volume XXV, 1955, p. 9.
[74] H.M. Colvin, *The history of the King's works: 1600-1782*, Volume V, 1976, pp. 350-54.
[75] Ibid.

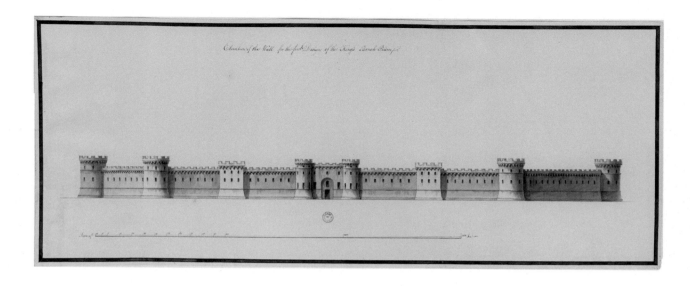

Fig 18. Adam office, design for a curtain wall to enclose King's Bench Prison, 1773. SM Adam volume 38/21. Photograph: Ardon Bar-Hama

in 1773 (Figs 17-18). These included an extension to the lodgings and a new castle-style curtain wall to improve security. 'The castle style was eminently suited to prisons, although in a reversal of the defensive role the walls were to keep people in rather than out', wrote Stephen Astley, adding that it was 'completely medieval in style, almost defensible, and suitably terrifying'.[76]

Adam's designs for the King's Bench Prison were not executed. Instead an extension was erected under the supervision of William Robinson, succeeded in 1775 by Kenton Couse, but within weeks of completion in 1780 a large portion of the prison was destroyed by fire during the Gordon Riots. This prompted Couse to rebuild to the same design in 1780–81, while making some improvements to the structural fabric.[77] In the 1840s the Prison was merged with the Fleet and Marshalsea Prisons, and was renamed the Queen's Bench. It was finally closed in 1869 when the Debtors Act limited the number of people that could be committed to prison for debt.[78] In 1879 the building was sold for demolition.

Lloyd's Coffee House, Cornhill

In the 1680s a coffee house was established by Edward Lloyd in Tower Street, moving in 1692 to Abchurch Lane, and this became a popular meeting place for ships' captains, owners and merchants to exchange shipping news and negotiate marine insurance. The most respectable

[76] S. Astley, *Robert Adam's Castles*, 2000, pp. 34-35.
[77] Colvin, 2008, p. 281.
[78] SoL, Volume XXV, 1955, p. 13.

among this group broke away in 1769 and founded the New Lloyd's Coffee House in Pope's Head Alley, but the success of the business was such that within only two years the new site proved too small and 79 merchants subscribed £100 each towards new premises.[79] Adam was commissioned to design a new building, probably intended for Freeman's Court off Cornhill.[80]

Seven Adam office drawings for Lloyd's survive at the Soane Museum. The design takes the form of a Roman basilica, being an apsidal rectangle of 71 by 20 feet. In the 1960s Damie Stillman noted that 'Adam's delight in spatial arrangements and elegant decoration was not restricted to domestic architecture'.[81] This commission allowed Adam to work on an interior which was of a scale larger than the rooms in even the grandest country house. His proposed interior was extremely opulent, making use of scagliola for the shafts of the screen columns and

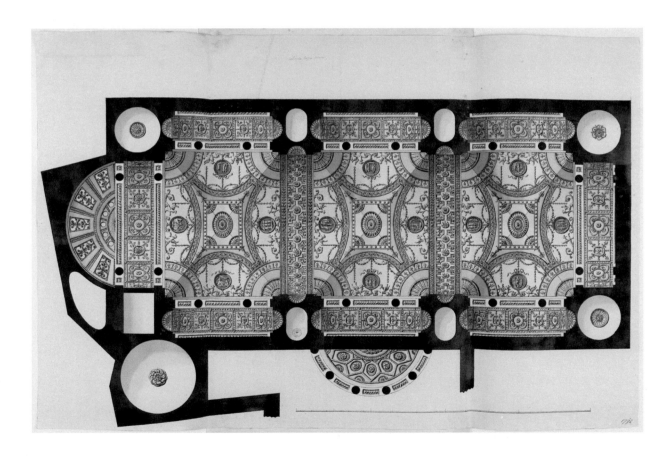

Fig 19. Adam office, design for the ceiling of Lloyd's Coffee House ceiling, 1772. SM Adam volume 12/120. Photograph: Ardon Bar-Hama

[79] Weinreb, 2008, pp. 491-92.
[80] King, 2001, Volume 2, p. 57.
[81] Stillman, 1966, p. 73.

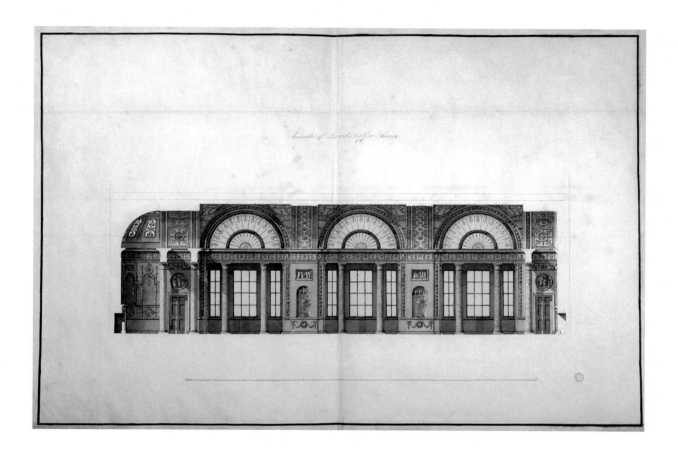

Fig 20. Adam office, design for the interior of Lloyd's Coffee House, 1772. SM Adam volume 30/60.
Photograph: Geremy Butler

dense ornamentation to the colourful walls and ceiling (Figs 19-20). His sectional drawing for the scheme show his characteristic linear decoration of the 1770s, as well as multiple screened apses which he used throughout his career. Such extensive ornamentation would have been expensive and it was perhaps owing to the projected cost that the scheme was not executed.

Instead of Adam's building, in 1774 Lloyd's took rooms in the Royal Exchange. It was not until the twentieth century that Lloyd's of London – by then a formal society of underwriters – commissioned a bespoke building for their offices: in 1925–28 they built at 12 Leadenhall Street to designs by Sir Edward Cooper, and a further building was erected in 1950–58 at 51 Lime Street to designs by Terence Heysham. More recently both of these buildings have been replaced: Cooper's 1920s building was demolished in 1986 and replaced to designs by Richard Rogers, and Heysham's 1950s building was demolished in 2004 and replaced with the Willis Building to designs by Lord (Norman) Foster.[82]

[82]   Weinreb, 2008, p. 492.

Lloyd's of London are undoubtedly aware of their connection with Adam. In 1955, when the Marquess of Lansdowne decided, controversially, to demolish most of Bowood House, Wiltshire, Lloyd's purchased the interior of Adam's 1763 'great room' there.[83] However, what was recreated in the board room at Lime Street was not the original room but a smaller adaptation, as many of the fixtures and fittings were not included (such as the windows, shutters, architraves, chair rail and skirtings). Other fragments had been kept in storage, and when the room was moved to the Rogers building on Leadenhall Street in 1983–86, to serve as the Lloyd's Council Room, these were reused, along with some replica items, to recreate the room nearer to its original size and form. It remains a remarkable survival from an Adam country house in the most unexpected of places.

Aldersgate Street

Now a short portion of the A1, Aldersgate Street was named after one of the Roman city gates, and the first building to be recorded here in 1135 was the church of St Botolph Aldersgate. Particularly during the Elizabethan period, the street was populated by a mix of nobility and the merchant classes. Following heavy bombing in the Second World War, Aldersgate Street has been largely rebuilt.[84]

152 Aldersgate Street

The origins of 152 Aldersgate Street are not known, but in the eighteenth century it was the home and business premises of Alderman the Hon. Thomas Harley, the fourth son of the 3rd Earl of Oxford. He served as MP for the City of London in 1761–64 and Herefordshire in 1776–1802, as well as being an Alderman of London in 1761–1804, Sheriff of London in 1763–64 and Lord Mayor of London in 1767–68. Harley established himself as a wine merchant on Aldersgate Street around 1752 and within a decade had branched out into clothing and military contracts, a business which during the American War of Independence became extremely lucrative.[85] In 1778 he went into a banking partnership with Sir Charles Raymond, forming 'Raymond, Harley, Webber and Co.' on George Street, affording him the wealth to purchase an estate near Leominster, Herefordshire, and to build Berrington Hall in 1778–81 to designs by Henry Holland.[86]

In 1752 Harley married Anne Bangham, the daughter of Edward Bangham MP, with whom he had two sons and five daughters, and in 1781 their second daughter, Sarah Harley, married Robert, 10th Earl of Kinnoull, the son of Archbishop Robert Hay-Drummond, who was Adam's patron at Brodsworth Hall, South Yorkshire c.1761–65.[87] It was not, however, through this connection that Adam came to Harley's attention, as it was a decade before the Kinnoull marriage in 1771 when he was employed to make interior decorative designs for 152 Aldersgate Street.

[83] Harris, 2001, p. 110.
[84] Weinreb, 2008, p. 14.
[85] *History of Parliament* online (hereafter HoP): Hon. Thomas Harley: http://www.historyofparliamentonline.org/volume/1754-1790/member/harley-hon-thomas-1730-1804 (accessed 11/08/2016).
[86] Colvin, 2008, p. 529.
[87] Bolton, 1922, Volume II, Index p. 74.

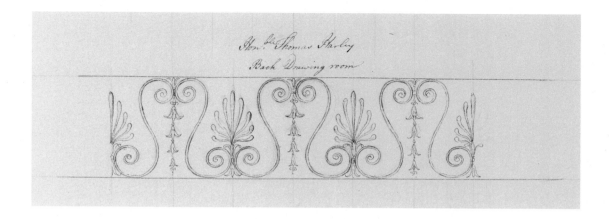

Fig 21. Attributed to James Adam, frieze for the back parlour of 152 Aldersgate Street, n.d. SM Adam volume 53/27 (detail). Photograph: Ardon Bar-Hama

Five drawings survive for the house, showing three simple ceiling designs, a console chimneypiece design and an attractive frieze design composed of drops of calyx alternating with anthemia and supported and connected by strigil-shaped arabesques. The frieze is inscribed as being for the back drawing room (traditionally the rear room on the first floor of a terraced house) and it is possible that one of the ceilings and the chimneypiece were also for that location (Fig. 21). However, for reasons unknown, none of Adam's designs for Harley were executed. The twentieth-century rebuilding of Aldersgate Street included a large office building at No. 50 which encompasses the plot of Harley's former house.

Lincoln's Inn

One of the four present Inns of Court, Lincoln's Inn was founded in the fourteenth century on land gifted by Henry de Lacy, 3rd Earl of Lincoln.[88] The Earl's heraldic lion rampant appears in the arms of the Society of Lincoln's Inn, which can be seen on two of the gated entrances to its large complex, built gradually over the centuries. The earliest surviving element is the Old Hall of 1489–92. The Old Buildings were constructed in c.1490–1520; New Square was built in 1682–93, and more recently the New Hall and Library were added in 1843–5.[89]

In 1771 the Society of Lincoln's Inn established a competition to design a building for their plot between Chancery Lane and Lincoln's Inn Fields, incorporating the existing chapel and providing chambers for barristers and benchers. Rival designs were submitted by Adam, Matthew Brettingham the younger, James Paine and Sir Robert Taylor. Adam's designs survive

[88] B. Cherry and N. Pevsner, *The buildings of England: London 4: North*, 1998, p. 284.
[89] Weinreb, 2008, p. 485.

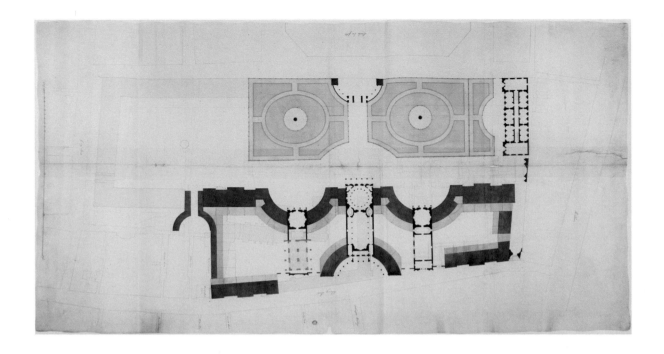

Fig 22. Adam office, plan for rebuilding at Lincoln's Inn, 1772–74. SM Adam volume 28/15. Photograph: John Bridges

at the Soane Museum, while those by Brettingham, Paine and Taylor, thought to have been lost, were rediscovered in a cellar beneath Lincoln's Inn in 1988.[90]

Adam's design comprises a vast complex of interconnecting ranges, with curved façades to both Chancery Lane and Lincoln's Inn Fields, all in the manner of the grandest of country houses (Fig. 22). However, there is an unusual density of windows in order to provide for the numerous small offices required within a building of this type. It has been suggested that Adam's extensive scheme was intended to catch the eye of the Society and that he had intended to submit a more modest and affordable version later, as suggested by a small pencil-drawn variant on his plan.[91] The rooms on Adam's plan are not labelled but it is likely that the large circular rooms were intended as libraries or record repositories.[92] The central colonnaded circular room is reminiscent of Adam's contemporary design for the rotunda within the Edinburgh Register House. The large central rectangular apsidal hall was probably intended for ceremonial purposes and the pre-existing chapel is identifiable within the western cross range from the footprint of the undercroft in pink. On the side facing Lincoln's Inn Fields Adam had intended to construct a piazza.

[90]   R. Hradsky 'The 1771 competition for rebuilding Lincoln's Inn', *The Georgian Group Journal*, 2009, pp. 95-106.
[91]   Ibid., p. 102.
[92]   A. Rowan, *'Bob the Roman', heroic antiquity & the architecture of Robert Adam*, 2003, p. 30.

A year after the competition was established – and after Brettingham and Paine had already submitted their designs – the Society additionally requested offices for the six clerks responsible for the Chancery Court, who themselves employed a further 60 clerks for the administration of Lincoln's Inn.[93] Adam's scheme for this addition was characteristically extravagant, comprising a two-storey, fifteen-bay building in the north-east corner of Lincoln's Inn Fields, lavishly ornamented with a rusticated basement, pediment, relieving arches and sculpture.

Unsurprisingly, Adam's grandiose proposal was too ambitious and it was Taylor's more affordable design which won the Society's favour. Indeed, Taylor's clerks' office was cleverly inserted within the main building rather than emulating Adam's additional block. Taylor's scheme was partly executed in 1774–80, and came to be known as Stone Buildings, as the principal (west) front is clad in stone.[94] The south end of the west wing was completed in 1842–45 by Philip Hardwick to a slightly modified design, and the whole survives largely as built.[95] Adam's scheme would have created the broadest classical façade in Britain, but it was never realistic in either scale or cost. Despite this, the Adam office competition drawings include some of the finest perspective views to survive from the eighteenth century (Figs 23-24). Such

Fig 23. Adam office, view of the proposed façade at Lincoln's Inn facing Chancery Lane, 1772–74. SM Adam volume 28/14. Photograph: Ardon Bar-Hama

[93]   King, 2001, Volume 2, p. 38.
[94]   Colvin, 2008, p. 1025.
[95]   Ibid., p. 479.

Fig 24. Adam office, view of the proposed façade at Lincoln's Inn facing Lincoln's Inn Fields, 1772–76. SM Adam volume 28/13. Photograph: Hugh Kelly

perspectives were usually only produced by Adam for publication, but in this case he was using every weapon in his armoury to impress upon the Society – whose members may not have been architecturally literate enough to understand his plans and orthogonal elevation drawings alone – that his scheme was magnificent beyond imagining.

Southampton Row

Forming part of a principal artery through London, Southampton Row now connects High Holborn to the south and Russell Square to the north, but in the eighteenth century it gave access to fields on the northern boundary of the city. Previously known as Kingsgate Street, it was renamed in the seventeenth century after Thomas Wriothesley, 4th Earl of Southampton, Lord Treasurer under Charles II.[96]

---

[96]   ODNB: 6th Duke of Bolton: http://www.oxforddnb.com/view/article/30077?docPos=3 (accessed 3/08/2016).

Bolton House, 26 Southampton Row (later 66-67 Russell Square)

Situated on the Bedford Estate, at the northern end of Southampton Row, No. 26 was leased in 1770 by Harry Paulet, 6th Duke of Bolton, who had succeeded his brother Charles five years previously. Despite this inheritance, Bolton had continued his distinguished career in the Royal Navy, rising to the rank of Admiral of the Blue in the same year that he acquired the house – and then to Admiral of the White in 1775.[97]

The house had been built in 1759–63 for Frederick Calvert, 4th Baron Baltimore, probably to designs by John Vardy. Vardy had worked for Baltimore before, producing designs for his country seat, Woodcote Park, Surrey, in about 1755. He had also worked for Bolton's brother, the 5th Duke, in 1761–63, remodelling the south front of the family's country seat, Hackwood Park, Hampshire.[98] 26 Southampton Row became available following Baltimore's trial for rape in 1768, when, despite his acquittal, he fled to Italy.[99]

Although the house was relatively new, Bolton immediately commissioned additions and new interiors. Vardy had died in 1765 and so Bolton turned to Adam, who transformed the conventional Palladian house into a stylish neoclassical one and completed the scheme in 1777. There are thirty extant drawings for these works at the Soane Museum. These include Adam's executed ceiling designs for the hall, the Duke and Duchess's dressing rooms, the ante-room, and the drawing room; chimneypiece designs for the library and drawing room and designs for various items of furniture, including a set of mirror frames for the drawing room. Adam's vibrant 1770 design for the ceiling of the Duchess's dressing room is a variant of the vault in the Crypt of Lucina at the Cemetery of St Calixtus near Rome (*c.* 220 AD) and is ornamented with medallions attributed to Angelica Kauffman (Fig. 25).[100] The arrangement of a circle within an octagonal frame proved immensely influential and recurs in many other Adam ceiling designs of the 1770s, including that for the glass drawing room at Northumberland House (see p. 15).

The drawing room was in the north-east corner of the house facing the garden, on the first floor adjacent to the Duchess of Bolton's dressing room. It was remodelled by Adam in 1772–73, including a selection of gilt mirror frames, and became the most opulent interior within the house (Fig. 26). Adam's design for the principal mirror frame was intended to fill the entire south wall, and was ornamented with armorial hounds: a unifying motif also found in the overdoors, frieze and chimneypiece. Furthermore, in 1773 Adam designed a magnificent commode for the room, a design which was later modified for a pair of commodes in the drawing room at Osterley, the home of the banker Robert Child.[101] Immediately following his work on Bolton House, Adam was commissioned by Bolton to make designs for Hackwood Park.

After Bolton's death in 1794 the lease of 26 Southampton Row was acquired by another of Adam's patrons, Alexander Wedderburn, 1st Earl of Rosslyn, for whom Adam had worked at Mitcham Grove, Surrey. Six years later, in 1800, Russell Square was laid out by the 5th Duke of Bedford, with the square directly west of the house. Further changes were wrought by Rosslyn

[97] Ibid.
[98] Colvin, 2008, p. 1075.
[99] E. Harris, 'Robert Adam on Park-Avenue – the interiors for Bolton house', *Burlington*, February 1995, p. 68.
[100] Stillman, 1966, p. 34.
[101] Beard, 1978, p. 54.

Fig 25. Adam office, design for the ceiling of the Duchess of Bolton's dressing room at Bolton House, 1770. SM Adam volume 12/35. Photograph: Ardon Bar-Hama

himself, who in 1803 divided the property into three separate dwellings, Nos 66 and 67 Russell Square and a house behind known as Bolton Gardens.[102]

During the nineteenth century, No. 66 became home to the Royal Society of Photographers and No. 67 to the lawyer and poet Sir Thomas Talfourd. Bolton Gardens was rebuilt at the turn of the twentieth century for use by the National Union of Teachers, which also acquired No. 67, but this was short-lived as both Nos 66 and 67 were purchased for the site of the Imperial Hotel in 1910, and finally demolished in 1913. The Adam ceiling for the Duchess's dressing room and the chimneypiece from the drawing room were purchased for Percy Pyne's neo-Georgian mansion at 680 Park Avenue, New York, built in 1909–11 by McKim, Mead and White.[103] The Imperial Hotel was built as a sister hotel to the adjacent Hotel Russell, both to designs by

[102] Harris, 1995, p. 74.
[103] Ibid., pp. 68-75.

Fig 26. Adam office, design for a mirror frame for the southern wall of the drawing room at Bolton House, 1772. SM Adam volume 20/84. Photograph: Ardon Bar-Hama

Charles Fitzroy Doll. This original hotel building was demolished in 1966. Its replacement, designed by C. Lovett Gill and Partners, opened in 1969 and remains *in situ* on the former site of Bolton House.[104]

[104]   Cherry, 1998, p. 326.

Soho Square

A short distance from the intersection of Oxford Street and Charing Cross Road, Soho Fields was granted to Henry Jermyn, Earl of St Albans, by Charles II, and St Albans quickly leased the land for development.[105] In 1677–91 Soho Square – originally known as King Square – was created when forty-one houses were built around Soho Fields by Richard Frith, a bricklayer, and Cadogan Thomas, a timber merchant. Initially popular with the aristocracy, the square contained several large houses, but by 1770 most of these residents had moved and it was no longer a fashionable area. In the nineteenth century Soho Square became a commercial area and largely remains as such.[106]

20 Soho Square

The Hon. John Grant was a lawyer and the eldest son of the Scottish judge Patrick Grant, Lord Elchies. A Baron of the Court of Exchequer in Scotland, he owned a sugar plantation in Granada, the income from which enabled him to acquire the original seventeenth-century house at No. 20 in 1771. Situated on the east side of the square, this was a three-storey, five-bay house, but shortly after its construction the neighbouring two-bay house was incorporated into it to form a very generous single dwelling for Oliver Cromwell's son-in-law, Thomas Belasyse, 1st Earl of Fauconberg, who lived there in 1689–1700. This uniting of two houses into one resulted in uneven fenestration, with the two southern bays being more widely spaced than their five northern counterparts. Following Lady Fauconberg's death in around 1713 the lease passed through various hands until it was sold on the death of the 4th Duke of Argyll in 1770 to Baron Grant.[107]

Grant then consulted Adam about refacing the house and providing new interiors, perhaps as a counterbalance to Soho Square having fallen out of fashion. Twenty-seven drawings showing Adam's designs survive at the Soane Museum. Various potentially expensive alterations were not made, including a scheme for an additional wing connecting to a new stable. However, Adam's scheme to reface the front facing Soho Square was executed, with a rusticated basement surmounted by eight pilasters – Corinthian in Adam's design but Ionic in execution – which articulated the bays across the first and second floors (Fig. 27). This did nothing to even out the fenestration but it did draw attention away from it.

Furthermore, Adam made designs for an interior with variously shaped rooms and lively neoclassical decorative schemes. Being such a large townhouse, Adam was not constrained by the typical terraced house arrangement and on the first floor he created oval, square and apsidal drawing rooms as well as Grant's bedroom. Below on the parlour (ground) floor he installed an eating room, dressing room and oval parlour. Drawings survive for at least one element of each room, including ceiling designs of 1771–72, such as that for the square drawing room arranged in a curving X-shape around a central medallion; this is known to have been executed as it appears in a painting of the room by J. P. Emslie. It is not known how many of Adam's other

---

[105] Weinreb, 2008, p. 848.
[106] Bradley, 2003, pp. 426-27.
[107] SoL, Volume XXXIII, 1966, p. 69.

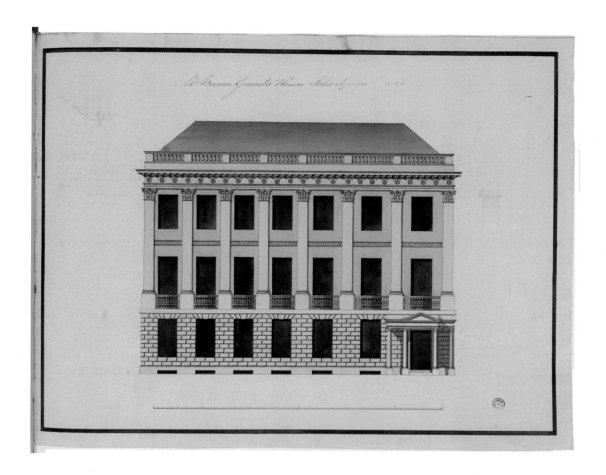

Fig 27. Adam office, design for the façade of 20 Soho Square, 1771. SM Adam volume 42/48. Photograph: Ardon Bar-Hama

interior designs for 20 Soho Square were executed as there was large-scale redecoration in the nineteenth century. However, certain elements are known to have come to fruition, such as Adam's ceiling design for the apsidal third drawing room. This had painted panels by Angelica Kauffman and Biagio Rebecca, which survived *in situ* until *c.*1905–6 when the then owner of the property transported them to his house at Bushey, Hertfordshire.[108]

Despite his wealth, the cost of Adam's works at 20 Soho Square required Grant to take a mortgage on the property in 1773 and a few months later he moved out. The house stood empty for a decade as the square was no longer fashionable. No. 20 was eventually sub-let as John Wright's Hotel and Coffee House (later the Crown Coffee House and Tavern), and then in 1810 it became the premises of a musical instrument maker. In 1858 it was taken by Messrs

[108] Ibid.

Fig 28. Adam office, design for the ceiling for the square drawing room at 20 Soho Square, 1771. SM Adam volume 12/109. Photograph: Ardon Bar-Hama

Crosse & Blackwell, oilmen and salters (already in ownership of No. 21), and in 1924 it was demolished to make way for a new high-rise block for Crosse & Blackwell, built in 1924–26 by Messrs Joseph.[109] That building remains in use as offices.

Charlotte Street

Running south from Percy Street, and parallel to Tottenham Court Road, Charlotte Street was named after George III's wife Queen Charlotte. In the late 1760s seventeen houses were built here by the Duke of Bedford to designs by Stiff Leadbetter.[110]

[109] Bradley, 2003, p. 428.
[110] C. Wainwright, '"The distressed poet" and his architect: George Keate and Robert Adam', *Apollo*, January 1996, p. 39.

9 Charlotte Street (later 18 Bloomsbury Square)

No. 9 was one of Leadbetter's houses. It was home to George Keate a writer, painter and collector of coins, cameos, gems, shells, minerals and insects. He began his career as a clerk, entering the Inner Temple in 1751, but owing to great personal wealth was never beholden to his legal career.[111] A Grand Tour followed in 1754–57, during the course of which he met Robert Adam in Rome. On marrying Jane Catherine Hudson in 1769, Keate moved from the Inner Temple to his newly completed townhouse at 9 Charlotte Street.[112]

In 1772 Adam was commissioned to provide new interiors, and in 1777 Keate acquired additional land to the rear of the property, enabling Adam to design an octagonal extension, probably to serve as Keate's museum.[113] Twenty-two drawings for the house survive at the Soane Museum, and these include ceilings for the dining room, dressing room and octagon room, glass frames, girandoles and furniture.

It is not known which of Adam's designs for the house were executed,

Fig 29. Adam office, design for a display table for 9 Charlotte Street, 1777. SM Adam volume 17/33. Photograph: Ardon Bar-Hama

but we do know that at least one of his ceiling designs came to fruition, as in 1787 Keate wrote *The Distressed Poet: a serio-comic poem*, in which he described taking Adam to court because a ceiling to his design had collapsed. Keate lost his suit and Adam was awarded £163 14s 4d in 1786.[114] The ceiling in question was described as Etruscan in style, and while none of Adam's extant ceiling designs for the house make use of the characteristic black and terracotta Etruscan colour scheme, there was an Etruscan-style overmantel mirror frame designed for the octagonal room, as well as an Etruscan-coloured display table (Fig. 29) – which was sold at auction after

[111] ODNB: George Keate: http://www.oxforddnb.com/view/article/15217 (accessed 22/08/2016).
[112] Wainwright, 1996, p. 39.
[113] Ibid., p. 41.
[114] Ibid., p. 44.

Keate's death and survives in a private American collection – so the ceiling in question was most likely in the octagonal museum room. One can only imagine what damage the collapsed ceiling did to Keate's collection.

Adam also designed a ceiling and frieze executed for an unknown Mr Lyte in the neighbouring house at No. 8 Charlotte Street (now 10 Bloomsbury Street) in 1773. The designs for Lyte have previously been conflated as part of the project for Keate,[115] but this is incorrect. Unlike No. 8 Charlotte Street for Mr Lyte, which survives with Adam's ceiling intact and is used as offices, Keate's house at No. 9 was destroyed in the Blitz.[116]

Mansfield Street and New Cavendish Street

The Portland Estate originally comprised land sold by James I in the Manor of Tyburn, in what is now Marylebone. It passed through various hands until it came to the 2nd Duke of Portland by his marriage to Margaret Cavendish, daughter of the Earl of Oxford and Mortimer, under whom development of the estate had begun around 1719. The land was inherited in 1879 by the sister of the 5th Duke of Portland, Lucy, Baroness Howard de Walden, and it remains part of the Howard de Walden Estate.[117] Within its confines are found Mansfield Street and New Cavendish Street. A short street of terraced houses, Mansfield Street is situated to the north of Cavendish Square, running parallel to the southern end of Portland Place, and was built partly on the site of the Marylebone Basin, the York Building Company reservoir which had been intended to supply water to houses on the Cavendish–Harley Estate from 1725. In the event those houses were never built and the basin was filled in during the 1760s.[118]

New Cavendish Street, at the north end of Mansfield Street, was one of the main east–west streets built in the 1760s–80s running across Portland Place, between Great Portland Street and Harley Street. West of Harley Street this road was known at the time as Great Marylebone Street, while to the east of Great Portland Street it was known as Upper Marylebone Street; these were renamed as part of New Cavendish Street in 1904 and 1937 respectively.[119]

Mansfield Street

Mansfield Street was part of the Adam brothers' Portland Place development, for which they agreed to lease land from the Duke of Portland in 1767. As well as the short terrace of houses that was built at its north end, the street as laid out by the Adams also included a large detached mansion designed for Robert Adam's friend General Clerk at its south end (see p. 53). The street name commemorates one of the Portland family holdings in Nottinghamshire. Externally the terraced houses on Mansfield Street were relatively plain, built of brick and without extraneous ornamentation to the façades, but with elegant doorways flanked by Ionic

[115] Bolton, 1922 Volume II, Index pp. 36, 77.
[116] King, 2001, Volume 1, p. 317.
[117] Weinreb, 2008, p. 658.
[118] SoL, Volumes 51–52 (forthcoming). I am grateful to Colin Thom for allowing me to see his manuscript prior to publication.
[119] Weinreb, 2008, p. 577.

columns and surmounted by fanlights. However, things were very different inside, the Adam office providing numerous designs for elaborate interior decorations, including ceilings, chimneypieces and wall ornamentation.

Six houses, now Nos 5–15 (odd numbers) were built along the west side of the street, each three bays wide. These houses were equipped with a dining room or front parlour at the front on the ground floor, a back parlour behind, and two drawing rooms and a rear ante-room on the first floor. On the opposite side only four houses were erected, now Nos 16–22 (even numbers), and these are four bays wide.[120] These houses take the same form as their counterparts opposite, but have larger entrance halls and an additional front ante-room on the first floor. Each house had a courtyard and stables at the back.

The leases of the larger corner houses at the north end (now Nos 15 and 22) were retained by the Adam brothers as their own speculation, but the rest were taken by the craftsmen and builders involved in the construction in payment (or part payment) for their labour. Some of those involved were Thomas Nicholls, carver; Joseph Rose, plasterer; John Devall, mason; John Hobcraft, carpenter and builder; and William Grantham, another carpenter.[121] The houses were largely complete, or nearing completion by the time of the banking crisis in 1772 and their

Fig 30. Soane office, Royal Academy lecture drawing showing 11, 13 & 15 Mansfield Street, *c.*1806–15. SM 18/2/14. Photograph: Geremy Butler

[120]   King, 2001, Volume 1, p. 82.
[121]   Bolton, 1922, Volume II, Index pp. 41-42.

Fig 31. Adam office, design for the ceiling for the back drawing room at 7 Mansfield Street, 1772. SM Adam volume 13/59. Photograph: Ardon Bar-Hama

leases began to be sold on in 1773, mostly to aristocrats. The only houses which lagged behind were Nos 15, 16 and 22. No. 16 was not leased until 1776, and Nos 15 and 22 – the leases for which had been kept by the Adam brothers – were added to the Adelphi Lottery Sale of 1774 as prizes.[122]

There are no surviving Adam office plans or elevations for the fabric of the Mansfield Street terraced houses, but there is an early nineteenth-century Soane office Royal Academy lecture drawing showing an elevation of the street fronts of Nos 11, 13 and 15 (Fig. 30). The 35 surviving Adam office drawings for interior decorations at Mansfield Street are far from comprehensive, but they do include various ceiling designs, many of which were executed, as well as chimneypieces and a handful of designs for furniture (Fig. 31). All of the interior decorative schemes on Mansfield Street were neoclassical. Unfortunately, only eight of the Adam brothers' houses on Mansfield Street are represented within the surviving drawings, as there are no drawings for Nos 11 and 16.

Adam's Mansfield Street survives largely intact (Fig. 32). During the nineteenth century many of the houses had their first-floor windows cut down to floor level and ironwork balconettes

122 SoL, Volumes 51–52 (forthcoming).

Fig 32. Mansfield Street, 2016. Photograph: Lewis Bush

added; moreover, the ground floors of all the houses except for No. 20 were stuccoed and rusticated during the nineteenth century, and the rear stables of many have since been demolished.[123] On the west side of the street, Nos 5–13 survive, but No. 15 was severely damaged by damp, dry rot and requisitioning during the Second World War and was rebuilt as a facsimile of Adam's house in 1956–57. On the east side, Nos 16–22 survive, though Nos 16 and 22 were heavily rebuilt in the nineteenth and early twentieth centuries.[124] Within the remaining houses, original Adam interiors survive in parts, including both drawing room ceilings in Nos 5, 7, 9, 13 and 20.

Portland House, New Cavendish Street

William Henry Cavendish-Bentinck served as MP for Weobley, Herefordshire, for only a year until 1762, when he succeeded his father as the 3rd Duke of Portland and entered the House of Lords as a Whig. From this time he was extremely active in public life. From 1764 he took up the family sinecure as a Trustee of the British Museum; in 1765–66 he served as Lord Chamberlain;

[123]   King, 2001, Volume 1, p. 82.
[124]   SoL, Volumes 51–52 (forthcoming).

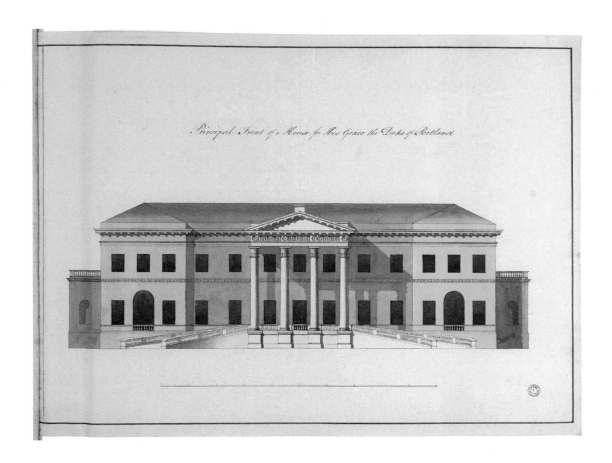

Fig 33. Adam office, design for the façade of Portland House, *c.*1770–76. SM Adam volume 29/2.
Photograph: Ardon Bar-Hama

in 1766 he became a Fellow of the Royal Society; in 1775 he became a Fellow the Society of Antiquaries; in 1782 he served as Lord Lieutenant of Ireland; in 1783 he served briefly as Prime Minister; in 1794 he was made a Knight of the Garter, and began his service as Home Secretary which lasted until 1801 and in 1807–9 he served again as Prime Minister, resigning only shortly before his death.[125]

Being an active public figure, Portland resided mostly in London. In 1766 he had married Lady Dorothy Cavendish, the daughter of the 4th Duke of Devonshire, enabling him to live at Devonshire House.[126] This was just as well, because his own London residence within the grounds of Whitehall – which had been leased by the family for around a century – was not only

[125] HoP: 3rd Duke of Portland: http://www.historyofparliamentonline.org/volume/1754-1790/member/bentinck-william-henry-cavendish-1738-1809 (accessed 3/08/2016).
[126] ODNB: 3rd Duke of Portland: http://www.oxforddnb.com/view/article/2162?docPos=2 (accessed 3/08/2016).

meagre, but under the terms of his father's will had been retained by his mother, the Dowager Duchess, with whom the Duke was in continual conflict, leaving him no option but to rent or borrow houses.[127] So when the Adam brothers began laying out Mansfield Street in the years around 1770, Portland commissioned Robert Adam to design him a large new palace – Portland House – located on an extensive plot on New Cavendish Street, facing towards Mansfield Street.[128]

We can see from eight surviving drawings at the Soane Museum that Adam proposed a building that was more on the scale of a country mansion than a London townhouse (Figs 33-34). At thirteen bays wide and set between a walled garden and a circular stable court, the scheme had a screen wall and gateway to New Cavendish Street. Adam's *grandiose hôtel* was presumably intended to emphasise Portland's political position and role as landlord to the Portland Estate. However, Portland House was never built. It is unlikely that the Duke could afford it. His fortune was limited by his mother's generous portion, and his electoral campaigns were costly; when in London

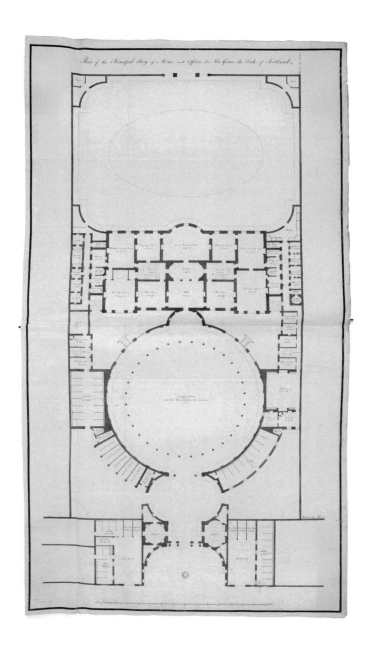

Fig 34. Adam office, plan for Portland House along with its stables and garden, *c.*1770–76. SM Adam volume 29/5. Photograph: Ardon Bar-Hama

[127] A. S. Turberville, *A History of Welbeck Abbey and its Owners*, vol.II, 1939, pp. 60, 63–65.
[128] Colvin, 2008, p. 637.

he lived mostly at Devonshire House. By 1805 he had surrendered the lease on the Whitehall house, which was then demolished, and at the time of his death in 1809 he was over £500,000 in debt.[129]

As late as February 1772 Adam provided the Duke with a price for the screen wall and gateway for Portland House (one of the office drawings in the Soane Museum has detailed measurements added to it). But by 1773 the scheme had been dropped, and in 1776 the vacant New Cavendish Street frontage was leased to John Johnson, who erected the present Nos 61 and 63 there. Both are still in reasonable repair: No. 61 is currently the location of the Energy Institute, No.63 is Asia House.[130]

Portland Place

Portland Place connects Regent's Park to the north and Regent Street and Oxford Circus to the south and is widely thought to be the finest street of Georgian London. Robert and James Adam agreed to lease the land for its construction from the Portland Estate in 1767, at the same time that the land for Mansfield Street was negotiated. But work on the Adelphi and Mansfield Street and increasing financial troubles held up progress in Portland Place until the 1770s.[131]

Adam had hoped that Portland Place would include some detached aristocratic palaces which might rival noblemen's urban homes on the Continent. There are surviving drawings for two such schemes from this early phase of work in the 1770s. These are designs for the Earls of Findlater and Kerry, each of whom had shown some interest in the concept. For Kerry's house Adam designed a sprawling five-block building, looking more like a country house than an urban palace, with a two-storey, five-bay central block, complete with a pediment and carriage ramps, flanked by two-storey, two-bay wings, and one-and-a-half-storey, five-bay pavilions (Fig. 35). Inside, Adam proposed a circuit of rooms including a library, dining room and two drawing rooms, arranged around a central circular ante-room lobed with alternating flat-backed and curving niches. Alistair Rowan has noted that the existence of six ceiling designs for Kerry's house suggests that the scheme was well advanced before its abandonment around 1774–75.[132] Such palaces were perhaps too ambitious and expensive, and in execution Portland Place remained a thoroughfare lined with blocks of three-storey terraced houses.

The magnificent width of the street is thanks to the legal requirement for the Adam brothers to leave a north-facing view towards Marylebone Farm from Foley House, which was located at the southern end of Portland Place on a plot now occupied by part of the Langham Hotel.[133] Foley House had been built c.1754–62 to designs by Stiff Leadbetter for Thomas Foley, 2nd Baron Foley of Kidderminster; it was demolished c.1815.[134]

[129] ODNB: 3rd Duke of Portland.
[130] SoL, Volumes 51–52 (forthcoming).
[131] Ibid.
[132] Rowan, 2007, p. 66.
[133] Weinreb, 2008, p. 658.
[134] Colvin, 2008, p. 637.

Fig 35. Adam office, design for a house for the Earl of Kerry on Portland Place, *c*.1769–73. SM Adam volume 48/95. Photograph: Ardon Bar-Hama

As in Mansfield Street (and at a later Adam speculation in London at Fitzroy Square), the leasehold interests of the various houses on Portland Place were allotted to the craftsmen responsible for the construction – for example the mason John Devall and the plasterer Joseph Rose junior.[135] Plans of how the exteriors should look, and designs for ceilings, friezes and chimneypieces were provided by the Adam office. Despite there being no surviving plan for the overall complex as built, there are over one hundred drawings at the Soane Museum for the neoclassical interior decorations, including 35 designs for ceilings, 68 for chimneypieces (Fig. 36), and 64 for friezes.

Constructed much like the houses on Mansfield Street but to a slightly larger scale, the Portland Place houses were divided into five blocks on each side of the road, with the central portion of each block slightly advanced and pedimented to offer variety. The width of each block was dictated not by a specific number of houses, but by the placement of the bisecting streets: Duchess, New Cavendish, Weymouth and Devonshire Streets. Building work began in 1774–75 with the blocks towards the southern end, while construction of the northern blocks was protracted over many years owing to a lack of funding and the building depression

[135]   Bolton, 1922, Volume II, Index pp. 46-47.

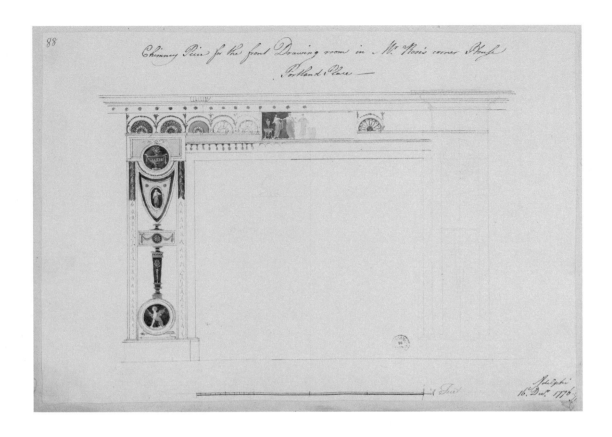

Fig 36. Adam office, design for a chimneypiece for the front room at 34 Portland Place, 1776. SM Adam volume 24/88. Photograph: Ardon Bar-Hama

brought about by the war with America.[136] In 1781, some six or seven years after construction began, forty-three houses appeared in the ratebooks, but thirteen of these were incomplete and untenanted.[137] The entire complex was designed with 32 houses on the west side of the road, and 36 houses on the east side. Portland Place was extended at its north end in the early nineteenth century when Park Crescent was undertaken by John Nash.

Many of the original Adam buildings on Portland Place survive with alterations and additional floors, new porches, new balconies and new glazing (Fig. 37). Survival of the original house in some form or other can be seen on the west side at the odd Nos 17-21, 27-47, 59-65 and 75, and on the east side at the even Nos 34-52 and 56-58. Adam interiors survive in a variety of conditions. The interiors of No. 33, now an events venue, are particularly fine. Quite amazingly, both drawing room ceilings survive in Nos 17, 19, 21, 31, 33, 34 and 48.[138] However,

[136] SoL, Volumes 51–52 (forthcoming).
[137] Ibid.
[138] King, 2001, Volume 1, pp. 88-92.

Fig 37. Portland Place, 2016. Photograph: Lewis Bush

the majority of these houses are in private ownership and cannot be visited, so instead we can simply enjoy the generous width of this pleasing tree-lined street.

Clerk House, Duchess Street

Sometimes known as No. 1 Mansfield Street, this large townhouse was built by Adam in 1768–71 for General Robert Clerk and his mistress, the wealthy Elizabeth, Countess of Warwick, the sister of Sir William Hamilton.[139] Its entrance was to the north, facing Duchess Street, and it was the first part of the Adam brothers' developments on the Portland Estate.[140]

[139] Ibid., p. 267.
[140] Weinreb, 2008, p. 250.

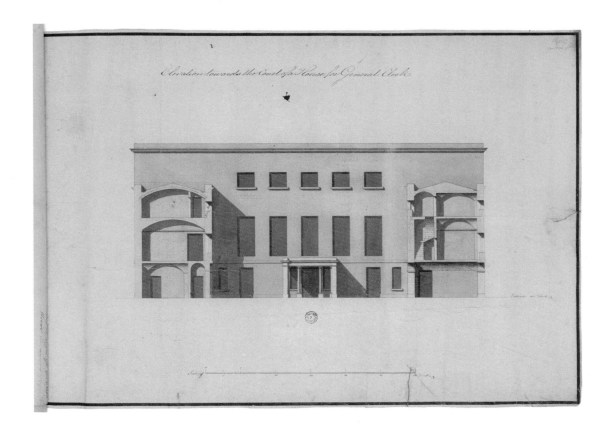

Fig 38. Adam office, design for Clerk House, *c.*1768. SM Adam volume 44/3. Photograph: Ardon Bar-Hama

The son of an Edinburgh physician and friend of the Adam brothers, Robert Clerk was an army officer involved in the War of the Austrian Succession and the Seven Years' War. His lengthy affair with the Countess led to her separation from her husband, the Earl of Warwick, and hence the commissioning of a new house from Adam. The pair finally married in 1774, the Earl having died the previous year. Although their new house was basically complete by around 1771, it was not occupied until 1774, when it was leased by the Clerks and James Adam to Sir Thomas Wynn of Glynllifon, Carnarvonshire (later Lord Newborough), who resided there until 1780. It was only after his departure that General Clerk and Lady Warwick finally took up residence.[141] Adam's surviving drawings for Clerk and Lady Warwick at the Soane Museum show a large but plain house, with a three-storey, five-bay façade with a projecting wing on each side to enclose an entrance court (Fig. 38). We can see on Adam's plan of the first floor that like his other grand townhouses, such as 23 Grosvenor Square or 20 St James's

141   C. Thom, 'Robert Adam's first Marylebone house: the story of General Robert Clerk, the Countess of Warwick and their mansion In Mansfield Street', *The Georgian Group Journal*, 2015, pp. 125–46.

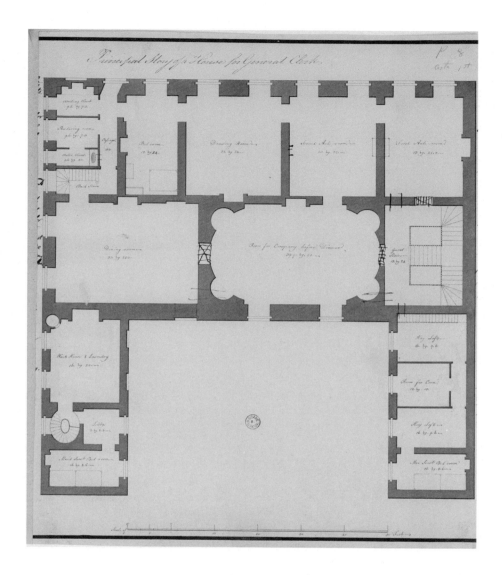

Fig 39. Adam office, plan for the first floor of Clerk house, *c*.1768. SM Adam volume 44/8. Photograph: Ardon Bar-Hama

Square, Clerk House had a circuit of rooms for entertainment (Fig. 39). There are also two surviving ceiling designs and a chimneypiece design for a drawing room, as well as a series of ornamental door panel designs.

Contemporary descriptions suggest that the fabric was executed in accordance with Adam's drawings, albeit with the room layout reversed from that on the plan.[142] The implementation

142 King, 2001, Volume 1, pp. 268-70.

of an Adam interior is less clear. Clerk House was purchased in 1799 by Thomas Hope, the celebrated collector of art, who redeveloped the building as a semi-public museum. In 1851 Hope's son sold the building for demolition.[143]

Chandos House, Queen Anne Street

In 1767 the Adam brothers entered into discussion with the Portland Estate concerning the development of Mansfield Street and Portland Place. The formation of these new streets resulted in an odd plot of land, 50 by 195 feet, behind General Clerk's house.[144] It was here in 1769–71 that the Adams built a grand, speculative townhouse facing Queen Anne Street.[145] A 99-year lease from 1767 was agreed in 1770, and James Adam took a mortgage on the property (the first of several) with Sir George Colebrooke in order to fund construction. The house was built with a facing of Scottish Craigleith stone, a rugged material more commonly used by the Adam brothers in Edinburgh.[146]

The only surviving Adam plans for Chandos House are for the ground and first floors and are in the care of the Cumbria Archive Service, Carlisle.[147] It is a large townhouse, with a library and a private apartment on the ground and first floors of a rear wing, allowing space in the main house for a circuit of reception rooms. It has been widely noted that this arrangement anticipated the layout of other, grander London townhouses by Adam, such as 20 St James's Square and 23 Grosvenor Square.

Eight drawings for the interior decorative schemes of the house are preserved at the Soane Museum and these include Adam's lively and colourful neoclassical ceiling designs for the eating room and parlour on the ground floor, the staircase, and the ante-room and front and rear drawing rooms on the first floor (Fig. 40). Perhaps the best element of Adam's interior decoration here is his ceiling for the front drawing room, which is divided into three compartments, with the largest, central compartment containing an X-shaped arrangement, further ornamented with Greek crosses, lunettes and painted panels by Antonio Zucchi.[148] The work was completed in 1772 when the house was placed for sale at Christie's, but no buyer was forthcoming until two years later in 1774, when the remainder of the lease was sold to James Brydges, 3rd Duke of Chandos.[149]

Prior to his succession to the Dukedom in 1771, Chandos had served as MP for Winchester in 1754–61 and Radnorshire in 1761–68, as well as being Lord of the Bedchamber in 1760–64, Lord Lieutenant of Hampshire in 1763–64 and 1771–80 and Lord Steward of the Household in 1783–89.[150] His sole heir, Lady Ann Eliza, married Richard, Earl Temple (created 1st Duke

[143] Weinreb, 2008, p. 250.
[144] T. Judith and S. Draper, 'Chandos House', *The Georgian Group Journal*, 1997, pp. 131-32.
[145] B. Cherry and N. Pevsner, *The buildings of England: London 3: North West*, 1991, p. 653.
[146] E. Harris, *The country houses of Robert Adam: from the archives of Country Life*, 2007, p. 151.
[147] Cumbria Archive Service DLONSL/11/9/6-7.
[148] Stillman, 1966, p. 102.
[149] Harris, 2007, pp. 152-54.
[150] HoP: James Brydges (1731-89): http://www.historyofparliamentonline.org/volume/1754-1790/member/brydges-james-1731-89 (accessed 16/08/2016).

Fig 40. Adam office, design for a ceiling for the front drawing room of Chandos House, 1771. SM Adam volume 13/55. Photograph: Ardon Bar-Hama

of Buckingham and Chandos in 1822).[151] Through this marriage, Temple inherited Chandos House on his mother-in-law's death in 1813 and two years later the house was sublet to the Austro-Hungarian Embassy, but on the expiration of the original lease in 1866, a new 99-year lease was acquired by Ann Eliza's grandson, the 3rd Duke of Buckingham and Chandos.[152]

The 3rd Duke made various alterations, including the amalgamation of Adam's ground-floor rooms in the rear wing to create a new dining room. Adam's friezes in the back parlour and drawing rooms were damaged at this time and plaster alternatives were substituted.[153] When the 3rd Duke died in 1889, the lease passed to his nephew, the 4th Earl Temple. Temple died in 1902 and the lease passed through various hands, until 1963 when a new 99-year lease was acquired by the Royal Society of Medicine, only to be sold again in 1986 to finance the

[151] Bolton, 1922, Volume II, Index p. 36.
[152] Harris, 2007, p. 154.
[153] Ibid.

Fig 41. Chandos House, 2016. Photograph: Lewis Bush

refurbishment of their principal building at 1 Wimpole Street. Unfortunately, the lease of Chandos House then passed in 1990 to an investment company who left the house empty for five years, resulting in considerable damage: during this period many of Adam's original chimneypieces were stolen, and the building fabric was badly damaged by extensive dry rot and water ingress. English Heritage placed Chandos House on the 'Buildings at Risk' register in 1994, issuing a repairs notice to the leaseholder in 1996 and a compulsory purchase order three months later. Happily, Chandos House was saved in 2002 when the Howard de Walden Estate (the freeholders) bought out the leaseholder and undertook a two-year programme of restoration work (Fig. 41).

Portman Square

Portman Square was laid out in 1764–84, on what was then the western edge of London – on land previously used for pig farming and the disposal of night soil. The landlord was Henry William Portman, and the houses were built to the designs of a variety of architects.[154]

20 Portman Square

20 Portman Square is a five-bay house, built for Elizabeth, Countess of Home from 1772 to designs by James Wyatt, with interiors by Robert Adam.[155] Elizabeth Gibbons was the daughter and heiress of a wealthy Jamaican merchant and plantation owner. In c.1720 she married James Lawes, the son of Sir Nicholas Lawes, Governor of the Island and another wealthy planter, but was widowed in 1733 and left a great fortune.[156] Little is then known of Elizabeth until 1742 when she married again, in London, the 8th Earl of Home – a renowned spendthrift – who abandoned her the following year, and she was widowed a second time when the Earl died in 1761.[157] By all accounts the Countess was a strong-minded and unusual lady: William Beckford reported that the 'riff raff' referred to her as the 'Queen of Hell'.

From 1771 the Countess is known to have lived temporarily at No. 43 on the south side of Portman Square (demolished 1964). In 1772, aged 68, she began to build a magnificent new house across the square at No. 20. It may seem strange that the Countess chose to rebuild at such an advanced age, but it has been widely suggested that this was connected with her niece's marriage in 1771 to HRH the Duke of Cumberland (see p. 125) and the Countess's desire to celebrate this advantageous union with 'receptions of quasi royal magnificence'.[158]

Wyatt's slow pace of work frustrated the Countess, and in 1775 he was replaced by Adam.[159] Adam's responsibilities were principally interior decoration, but some structural alterations did allow him to create a circuit of social spaces and his most successful urban stairwell: a top-lit

---

154 Cherry, 1991, p. 650.
155 Harris, 2001, p. 297.
156 L. Lewis, 'Elizabeth, Countess of Home, and her house in Portman Square', *Burlington Magazine*, August 1967, pp. 443-44.
157 M. Whinney, *Home House: 20 Portman Square*, 1969, p. 12.
158 Ibid., p. 11. Lewis, 1967, p. 450.
159 Harris, 2001, p. 300.

Fig 42. Adam office, design for the stairwell at Home House, *c*.1775. SM Adam volume 14/116.
Photograph: Ardon Bar-Hama

Fig 43. Adam office, design for the Etruscan dressing room at Home House, *c.*1777. SM Adam volume 14/132. Photograph: Ardon Bar-Hama

oval space with an Imperial staircase and dense ornamentation to the walls (Fig. 42). Adam's surviving drawings for the house at the Soane Museum – and indeed the extant building – show that he was responsible for a great many rooms including the music room (complete with an organ case), the drawing rooms, and an Etruscan-style dressing room (Fig. 43). The 1775–77 dates inscribed on Adam's drawings illustrate how determined the Countess was, as she took up residence in 1776 when much of the house was still unfinished.[160]

One of the drawing rooms at Home House was designed around a pair of portraits by Thomas Gainsborough of the Duke and Duchess of Cumberland. These had been exhibited at the Royal Academy in 1777. If it is true that the Countess built her house in support of her niece, these portraits represent the *raison d'être* of the house, and for them she commissioned Adam to design throne-like frames complete with Royal insignia (Fig. 44). In her will the Countess instructed

[160]   Whinney, 1969, p. 23.

Fig 44. Adam office, design for a frame for Gainsborough's portraits of the Duke and Duchess of Cumberland for Home House, 1777. SM Adam volume 20/162. Photograph: Ardon Bar-Hama

that the Gainsborough portraits be hung at the Mansion House unless the royal couple disapproved, in which case they should decide the fate of the paintings, and indeed, in 1809 the Duchess left the paintings to the Duke of Clarence (later William IV) and they are now part of the Royal Collection.[161]

The largest portion of the Countess's estate, including 20 Portman Square, was inherited by a nephew, William Gale, then still a schoolboy, and the house was leased to a succession of residents.[162] The Adam interiors in the house were restored in 1927–32 for Samuel Courtauld, who then passed the lease to the University of London for use by the Courtauld Institute of Art until 1989. From 1996 an eight-year restoration project began to convert the building – along with its neighbours to either side – into the exclusive Home House Club, including the recreation of Adam's organ case in the music room as a drinks cabinet.[163]

41 and 21 Portman Square

Two other houses on Portman Square for which the Adam office made designs were Nos 41 and 21, which belonged in succession to William Locke, an art connoisseur and patron. He is thought to have been the illegitimate son of William Locke, MP for Grimsby, from whom he may have inherited his fortune. He began collecting art during his Grand Tour in 1749, initially

[161] Lewis, 1967, p. 448.
[162] Ibid., p. 447.
[163] R. Simon 'All back to front: what happened to Home House when the Courtauld left', *The Spectator*, 5 June 1999, p. 50.

Fig 45. Adam office, design for a ceiling for the drawing room at 41 Portman Square, 1766. SM Adam volume 11/172. Photograph: Ardon Bar-Hama

housing the collection in London, but in 1774 he purchased Norbury Park, Surrey, where he lived until his death.[164]

Around 1764–65, when Portman Square was laid out, No. 41, on the south side, was leased by Locke – the first of three houses he acquired in the square. The origins of the house are unknown, but it is possible that the Adam office was involved. In 1765 James Adam was commissioned – possibly in collaboration with his brother Robert – to make designs for a house here. In the RIBA Drawings Collection are three surviving but unexecuted contract drawings for this house, designed and signed by James. It is not known if this design was for an entirely new house or merely for alterations to an existing one. There are also two surviving drawings at the Soane Museum, showing unexecuted designs for a drawing-room ceiling and a dressing-room chimneypiece, both dated 1766 (Fig. 45). None of James's interior decorative

---

[164] ODNB: William Locke: http://www.oxforddnb.com/view/article/16889?docPos=1 (accessed 3/08/2016).

designs for this house were executed, and it suffered damage during the Blitz. More recently the plot has been incorporated as part of No.40 Portman Square, offices and flats completed in 2008 to designs by Squires and Partners.[165]

In 1775–76 Locke gave up his lease of No. 41 in favour of a house he had commissioned at No. 21 on the north side of Portman Square. A relatively modest three-storey, three-bay house, this was built from around 1772 to designs by James Adam.[166] There are decorative interior designs at the Soane Museum, including some chimneypieces. If these were executed, however, they no longer survive.[167]

James Adam's house at No. 21 was altered in 1866 when the principal entrance was moved to its return flank on Gloucester Place, and again in 1972 when the interior was altered for the RIBA Drawings Collection.[168] More recently it has become part of the Home House Club (see p. 59). William Locke only remained at No. 21 for two years, owing to financial difficulties, and in 1778 he moved again, to No. 14 on the west side of Portman Square.[169] No designs from the Adam office are known to have been made for this third house and the plot is now part of Fitzhardinge House at Nos 12-14, a 1960s residential block.

Grosvenor Square

200 yards east of the Park Lane boundary to Hyde Park, Grosvenor Square – at 6 acres in size – is the second largest square in London.[170] It is the centrepiece of the 350-year-old Grosvenor Estate. The square was developed piecemeal, plot by plot, on land belonging to Sir Richard Grosvenor in 1725–31, so although only two of the original houses survive, there was never any great architectural uniformity.[171] It was an affluent residential square, and remained as such until the Second World War when it was largely requisitioned for the American military.

18 (later 19) Grosvenor Square

Nos 17-19 (now 18-20) on the north side of Grosvenor Square were built c.1725–29 as a single block to designs by Edward Shepherd and with a pedimented Palladian façade, representing one of the earliest attempts at a palace frontage to terraced housing. No. 19 was retained by Shepherd himself, but No. 18 was leased in 1730 by the 7th Earl of Thanet for £7,500, making it the most expensive house in the square.[172] It was then inherited by Sackville Tufton, 8th Earl of Thanet who succeeded his father in 1753. In 1767 the 8th Earl married Mary, daughter of Lord John Sackville, son of the Duke of Dorset, and had four sons, including the 9th, 10th and 11th Earls of Thanet.[173]

165 King, 2001, Volume 2, p. 130.
166 K. Maxwell, '21 Portman Square', *The Georgian*, Volume 1, 2005, p. 27.
167 King, 2001, Volume 1, p. 21.
168 Cherry, 1991, p. 650.
169 Bolton, 1922, Volume II, Index p. 48.
170 Bradley, 2003, p. 529.
171 Weinreb, 2008, p. 359.
172 Colvin, 2008, p. 920. SoL, Volume XL, 1980, pp. 133-36.
173 ODNB: 9th Earl of Thanet: http://www.oxforddnb.com/view/article/27802 (accessed 3/08/2016).

Fig 46. Adam office, design for a ceiling for the ground-floor dressing room at 18 Grosvenor Square, 1764. SM Adam volume 11/119. Photograph: Ardon Bar-Hama

Shortly after receiving the eight-year-old Mozart at 18 Grosvenor Square in 1764, Thanet commissioned Adam to design new interiors. Fourteen drawings survive at the Soane Museum for the gallery, the saloon, and the Earl's dressing room, all on the first floor, and for the dining room and the dressing room on the ground floor. The drawings include an executed design for the ceiling of the ground-floor dressing room (Fig. 46). This was converted into a morning room in the 1880s, but Adam's ceiling was preserved and is thought to have survived until the demolition of the house in 1933.[174] There is also a selection of surviving designs for mirror frames and girandoles, including a frame designed by James Adam in 1764 for the saloon (Fig. 47). This was executed but is now lost. The drawing itself is significant as Eileen Harris has noted: this was one of the earliest designs made by James following his return from the Grand Tour, and is the only design for furniture at the Soane Museum which is signed by him.[175]

[174] King, 2001, Volume 1, p. 308.
[175] E. Harris, *The furniture of Robert Adam*, 1963, p. 77.

Fig 47. Adam office, design for a mirror frame for
18 Grosvenor Square, 1764. SM Adam volume 20/3.
Photograph: Ardon Bar-Hama

Following his succession in 1786, the 9th Earl made alterations to the façade, possibly to designs by S.P. Cockerell, including the removal of the pediment. The 9th Earl then sold the lease in 1794 to the politician Paul Benfield and in the early 1800s the first-floor pedimented window dressings were removed. These were reinstated in a fairly confused way in the 1880s by a new tenant, Mrs Gerard Leigh, to designs by D. Cubitt Nichols.[176] Mrs Leigh also employed Frederick Arthur to renovate Adam's interiors and redecorate other rooms in an Adam revival style.[177]

In 1865 – following numerous alterations – the harmony of Shepherd's original block was destroyed when Nos 18 and 20 were demolished. In the 1930s a programme to rebuild the entire north side of the square was begun to designs by Fernand Billery. However, this was not completed until 1964, to a heavily modified design, the work having been delayed by the Second World War.[178]

23 (later 26) Grosvenor Square

Edward Smith-Stanley, MP for Lancashire, succeeded his grandfather as 12th Earl of Derby in 1776. His succession brought him the estate of Knowsley, Lancashire, as well as The Oaks, Surrey, via his aunt, Lady Charlotte Burgoyne. He maintained his ancestors' tradition of serving as Lord Lieutenant of Lancashire from 1776 until 1834, and was Chancellor of the Duchy of Lancaster in 1783 and 1806.[179] Derby is best remembered as a supporter of horse racing, but also for his troubled marriage.

---

[176] SoL, Volume XL, 1980, p. 136.
[177] Harris, 2007, p. 148.
[178] SoL, Volume XL, 1980, pp. 117, 136.
[179] HoP: Lord Edward Smith Stanley: http://www.historyofparliamentonline.org/volume/1754-1790/member/stanley-edward-1752-1834 (accessed 24/08/2016).

In 1774 Derby married Lady Elizabeth Hamilton, daughter of the 6th Duke of Hamilton and the famous beauty, Elizabeth Gunning, but after five years, the Countess conducted an affair with a notorious rake, John Frederick Sackville, 3rd Duke of Dorset, bringing a separation from Derby. He refused her a divorce – preventing her from marrying the Duke – and banned her from access to their three children. One week after the Countess's death in 1797, Derby married his companion, Miss Elizabeth Farren, an actress by whom he had another three children.[180]

The first Countess held considerable sway over Adam's work for Derby. To celebrate his marriage in 1774, Derby commissioned Adam to design a temporary pavilion at The Oaks, for a magnificent *fête champêtre* hosted by his uncle and aunt, General John Burgoyne and Lady Charlotte.[181] Derby later inherited Knowsley and The Oaks and commissioned Adam to make improvements to both houses in 1776 and 1777 respectively. At Knowsley, Adam designed a dairy for the enjoyment of the first Countess, but following her betrayal Derby had it demolished.[182] It was presumably through General John and Lady Charlotte Burgoyne that Derby met Adam, as they had been his patrons at 10 Hertford Street from 1769 (see p. 86). Excepting the Countess's dairy, few of Adam's designs for Knowsley and The Oaks were executed. Derby lost interest in building following the Countess's affair. His subsequent efforts were focused on horse racing and he founded the Epsom Oaks and the Derby Stakes.[183]

Prior to inheriting from his grandfather in 1775, Derby (then still Lord Stanley) resided at his London townhouse at 23 Grosvenor Square, affording him a convenient location for his political career. By the 1760s and 1770s there was widespread renovation work taking place in the square, its houses by then being some 50 years old. The Adam brothers worked on five houses in Grosvenor Square, including remodelling the interior of No. 23 for Lord Stanley.

A five-storey, three-bay terraced house, No. 23 was built *c*.1728 on the west side of Grosvenor Square under a 100-year lease belonging to Charles Griffith, a carpenter, who sold the lease in 1731 to Sir Robert Sutton for £6,500. The lease was acquired from Sir Robert in 1750 by James Smith-Stanley, Lord Strange, and inherited in 1771 by his son, Lord Stanley, then only nineteen years old. Two years later, Stanley approached Adam to redecorate the existing rooms in the house for his coming of age ball.[184] The rooms on the first floor were designed in 1773 and those on the ground floor – along with various furnishings – in 1774. Adam also built a Doric portico over the front door and a rear extension containing closets, waterclosets and a powdering room.[185] The works were closely supervised by Burgoyne.[186]

Adam's work at 23 Grosvenor Square – particularly in the third (great) drawing room with its ornamented groin vault and in the Countess's Etruscan-style dressing room – was some of his finest anywhere (Figs 48-49).[187] Many of the craftsmen who worked on the house are unknown, and the only artist associated with this interior, Antonio Zucchi, was mentioned by

[180] ODNB: 12th Earl of Derby: http://www.oxforddnb.com/view/article/47080?docPos=10 (accessed 24/08/2016).
[181] A. Rowan, Designs for castles and country villas by Robert & James Adam, 1985, p. 102.
[182] King, 2001, Volume 1, p. 342.
[183] ODNB: 12th Earl of Derby.
[184] SoL, Volume XL, 1980, p. 142.
[185] King, 2001, Volume 1, p. 298.
[186] SoL, Volume XL, 1980, p. 143.
[187] Stillman, 1966, p. 74.

Fig 48. Adam office, design for a ceiling for the great drawing room ceiling at 23 Grosvenor Square, 1773. SM Adam volume 12/144. Photograph: Ardon Bar-Hama

name in Adam's *Works in architecture.…*[188] Thomas Carter the younger is thought to have been responsible for various chimneypieces; and the japanned door panels have been attributed to Henry Clay.[189] Irrespective of the splendour and complexity of the scheme, Adam's office and associated craftsmen were under considerable pressure to complete the interior before Derby's wedding in 1774, but the work was not actually completed until a year later.[190] An incredible 94 Adam office drawings for the house survive at the Soane Museum. These include designs for ceilings, walls, friezes, chimneypieces, grates, glass frames, girandoles, curtain cornices, tables, seat furniture, a commode, a bed, carpets and door panels.

On his succession in 1851, the 14th Earl of Derby removed two chimneypieces, a mirror and two overdoor panels to his house in Stratford Place, Marylebone, and leased 23 Grosvenor

[188]   Adam, Volume II, 1779, preface.
[189]   SoL, Volume XL, 1980, p. 143. Y. Jones 'Japanner to His Majesty', *The Antique dealer and collectors guide*, January 1996, pp. 46-49.
[190]   SoL, Volume XL, 1980, p. 143.

Fig 49. Adam office, design for a chimneypiece and overmantel mirror frame for the Etruscan dressing room at 23 Grosvenor Square, 1774. SM Adam volume 23/51. Photograph: Ardon Bar-Hama

Place to the Dowager Duchess of Cleveland, on whose death in 1861 the house was demolished for rebuilding and the plot renumbered as 26. The house was rebuilt by the developer Sir Charles Freake, possibly to designs by Francis William Tasker. This was demolished in 1957 to make way for the American Embassy building, which spans the entire west side of Grosvenor Square, erected in 1957–60 to designs by Eero Saarinen.[191]

Hill Street

Crossing the boundary of the Berkeley and Grosvenor Estates, Hill Street extends south-west from Berkeley Square. It was mostly developed plot-by-plot in the late 1740s, with some of the original houses surviving *in situ* and now largely used as offices.[192]

23 (later 31) Hill Street

Dating to the initial development of Hill Street, No. 23 was commissioned by Elizabeth Montagu, the eldest daughter of Matthew Robinson, a landowner in Yorkshire. Elizabeth spent considerable time with her maternal grandmother, the wife of a Cambridge classics scholar, Dr Conyers Middleton, and it was probably there that she learned to appreciate intellectual pursuits. At that time she formed a friendship with Lady Margaret Harley (later 3rd Duchess of Portland), through whom Elizabeth was introduced to London and formed a strong desire for an elevated metropolitan lifestyle. In 1742 this was achieved when Elizabeth married Edward Montagu a grandson of the 1st Earl of Sandwich, owner of a country estate at Sandleford Priory, Berkshire, and valuable coal mines in Berkshire, Yorkshire and Northumberland. Moreover, Montagu shared Elizabeth's scholarly interests and was himself a mathematician.[193]

The Montagus spent much of the year in their London house at 23 Hill Street and it was here that Elizabeth established her reputation as a literary hostess, gathering around her a large group of intellectual friends, and earning the title 'queen of the bluestockings'. She took an active interest in the management of the family coal mines and increased their income to allow patronage and promotion of the arts and literature.[194]

The interior decoration of 23 Hill Street was largely designed by James 'Athenian' Stuart in 1760–72, but in 1766 Adam was commissioned to redecorate Elizabeth's dressing room on the first floor of the house.[195] This was known as the silver room and in reality was a feminine room for entertaining, which had been fitted up in the 1750s in a Chinoiserie style to Elizabeth's designs, with assistance from the poet Gilbert West.[196] Despite Elizabeth's patronage of Adam, he had limited experience of Chinoiserie; nonetheless the result was a beautiful neoclassical scheme with painted Chinoiserie motifs and medallions (Fig. 50).

---

[191] Ibid., p. 144.
[192] Weinreb, 2008, p. 402.
[193] ODNB: Elizabeth Montagu: http://www.oxforddnb.com/view/article/19014?docPos=1 (accessed 11/08/2016). E. Eger and L. Peltz, *Brilliant women: 18th-century bluestockings*, 2008, p. 24.
[194] Ibid., pp. 21-25.
[195] Colvin, 2008, pp. 49, 1002.
[196] Harris, 2001, p. 7.

Fig 50. Adam office, design for a ceiling for Elizabeth Montagu's dressing room at 23 Hill Street, 1766. SM Adam volume 11/200. Photograph: Hugh Kelly

There are six surviving drawings for Elizabeth Montagu's dressing room at the Soane Museum, one of which, showing the chimneypiece, has been attributed to Stuart. The others are the product of the Adam office and comprise: an exquisite design for the ceiling, which was executed with minor alterations; three designs for a carpet, which complement the ceiling but are not known to have been executed; and a design for an embroidered chair seat, presumably intended for the same room (Fig. 51). While there is no evidence that the seat was executed, it is interesting to note that the cabinetmaker William Linnell had been employed by Elizabeth Montagu to provide furniture for the house from 1752, including some black and gold japanned furniture for the dressing room which remains in the possession of the Montagu family's descendants.[197]

The most important element of Adam's work at 23 Hill Street was his ceiling. This is arranged around a large central fan – replaced in the nineteenth century with a circular medallion – and encircled by eight smaller Chinoiserie-style medallions, all set within a circular frame richly ornamented with guilloche, peltoid shields, festoons, bells, rosettes and strange pagoda-like leaves. This arrangement, composed of a ring of eight medallions, is inspired by copies after the antique, such as Francesco Bartoli's illustrations of ceilings at the Baths of Augustus in the Topham Collection, or Bernard de Montfaucon's *Supplement au livre de l'antiquité expliquée*, both of which were familiar to Adam.[198] Other examples of this arrangement within Adam's

[197] H. Hayward and P. Kirkham, *William and John Linnell: eighteenth-century London furniture makers*, 1980, p. 75.
[198] L. Gwynn and A. Aymonino. 'Paper palaces, surviving antiquity', *Eton College Collections Journal*, spring 2013, pp. 25-27.

Fig 51. Adam office, design for an embroidered chair seat for 23 Hill Street, *c.*1766. SM Adam volume 49/51. Photograph: Ardon Bar-Hama

work – both executed and unexecuted – can be seen in his designs for the ceilings of Lady Scarsdale's dressing room at Kedleston, the music room at Harewood, the dressing room at 15 Downing Street and the back drawing room at 10 Hertford Street, although none of these feature the delicate Chinoiserie motifs seen in Adam's design for Elizabeth Montagu.

The patroness seemed pleased with Adam's work, writing to her friend, the Duchess of Portland: 'Mr Adam came at the head of a regiment of artificers … The bricklayer talked about the alterations to be made in a wall, the stonemason was as eloquent about the coping of the said wall; the carpenter thought the initial fitting-up of the house not less important; then came the painter [Biagio Rebecca], who is painting my ceiling in various colours, according to the present fashion.'[199]

On Edward Montagu's death in 1775, Elizabeth was left a wealthy widow.[200] She acquired a 99-year lease on 22 Portman Square which she rebuilt in 1777–82 to designs by Stuart, and it was there that she famously gave roast beef and plum pudding to chimney sweeps and their apprentices on May Day each year. Unfortunately, Stuart's house at 22 Portman Square was lost to fire in 1941.[201] Adam's interior in the silver room at 23 Hill Street has been altered, with the circle of eight medallions in the ceiling now depicting the twelve signs of the Zodiac. It is not known when this alteration was made, but one scholar has suggested that the modification happened immediately after Adam's tenure, to designs by Stuart.[202] Either way, the altered ceiling survives *in situ* and the building is now used as offices.

[199] J. Lees-Milne, *The age of Adam,* 1947, p. 171.
[200] ODNB: Elizabeth Montagu.
[201] Colvin, 2008, p. 1002.
[202] D. Pullins, 'Reassessing Elizabeth Montagu's architectural patronage at 23 Hill Street, London', *Burlington*

31 (later 17) Hill Street

In the 1740s, the leases for eight houses on the south side of Hill Street were taken for development by Benjamin Timbrell.[203] One of these was No. 31, and later in the century it was the home of Sir Abraham Hume.

Sir Abraham Hume, 2nd Baronet of Wormleybury, Hertfordshire, was an avid collector of minerals and one of the founders of the Geological Society, as well as MP for Petersfield in 1774–80 and Hastings in 1807–18. He was born in Hill Street and inherited the house when he succeeded to his father's baronetcy in 1772.[204] In 1777–79 Hume commissioned Adam to provide new interiors for his country seat at Wormleybury, and at the same time asked him to make designs for alterations, interior decoration and furnishings for his townhouse on Hill Street.

Adam's designs for 31 Hill Street include ceilings for the staircase and drawing rooms, chimneypieces and grates, glass frames, girandoles, seat furniture (Fig. 52), candelabra, curtain

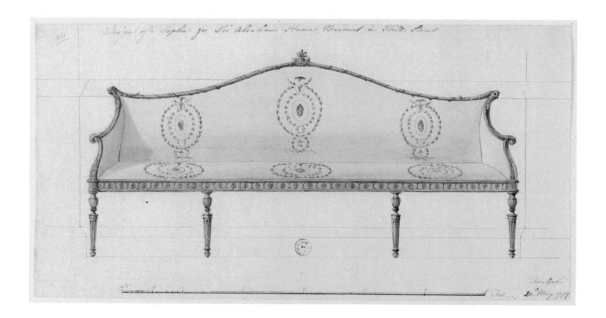

Fig 52. Adam office, design for a sofa for 31 Hill Street, 1779. SM Adam volume 17/84. Photograph: Ardon Bar-Hama

Magazine, June 2008, p. 402.
203   Bradley, 2003, p. 537.
204   HoP: Sir Abraham Hume: http://www.historyofparliamentonline.org/volume/1790-1820/member/hume-sir-abraham-1749-1838 (accessed 22/08/2016). ODNB: Sir Abraham Hume: http://www.oxforddnb.com/view/article/14131?docPos=2 (accessed 22/08/2016).

Fig 53. Adam office, design for the façade of 31 Hill Street, 1779. SM Adam volume 50/29. Photograph:
Ardon Bar-Hama

74

cornices, carpets, door furniture and various designs for ornamental panels. Sadly there are no surviving drawings for the rear wing which Adam added to the house, but his alterations to the façade can be seen in one of his drawings, including the articulation of the four floors (Fig. 53).

Now used as offices, the house survives as 17 Hill Street with some of Adam's interiors, but alterations were made for Charles Rube in 1906 to designs by Hindley and Wilkinson, including the addition of two further floors, an Ionic porch and new balconies on the first-floor windows.[205]

Berkeley Square

Located between Hyde Park and Green Park, Berkeley Square is named after the 1st Baron Berkeley of Stratton, a Royalist commander in the Civil War, who developed a large area north of Piccadilly following the Restoration.[206] Berkeley Square came about because the 3rd Lord Berkeley sold his house on Piccadilly in 1696 to the Duke of Devonshire, with the proviso that the vista to the north should be unobscured by future building. When developing the area from the 1730s onwards, the 4th and 5th Lords Berkeley maintained this vista to the north of Devonshire's house and the result was Berkeley Square.[207]

15 (later 38) Berkeley Square

On the west side of Berkeley Square, No. 15 was the townhouse of Robert Child, the second son of Samuel Child and the grandson of Francis Child, founder of the Child family banking dynasty. In the autumn of 1763 Robert Child succeeded his brother Francis as head of the family and the banking firm, as well as to his properties at Osterley and Upton Park. Child had been a partner in the bank since 1760 but following his succession is not known to have taken an active role in the business, serving instead as MP for Wells in 1766–82.[208]

15 Berkeley Square in fashionable Mayfair was purchased by Child in 1767 from the 4th Duke of Manchester for £10,000. Eileen Harris has suggested that Adam – already Child's architect at Osterley – acted as the 'go-between' in this sale as he was concurrently working for the Duke at Kimbolton Castle.[209] The family was previously in possession of a townhouse at 42 Lincoln's Inn Fields – purchased in 1702 – Child sold this in 1767 and most of its contents were removed to Osterley. Robert Child's own townhouse – before he succeeded his brother – was No. 59 Lincoln's Inn Fields, leased in 1762 in preparation for his marriage a year later, but having inherited from his brother this was sold in 1764 to his banking partner, Thomas Devon.[210]

As 15 Berkeley Square had been built in 1740, Child commissioned Adam to design new interiors for the drawing rooms and the principal bedchamber. It is likely that Adam installed

[205] Bradley, 2003, p. 538.
[206] Weinreb, 2008, p; 59.
[207] Bradley, 2003, p. 498.
[208] HoP: Robert Child: http://www.historyofparliamentonline.org/volume/1754-1790/member/child-robert-1739-82 (accessed 23/08/2016).
[209] E. Harris, 'The Childs in London' in T. Knox and A. Palmer, *Aspects of Osterley*, 2000, p. 37.
[210] Harris, 2000, pp. 35-37.

Fig 54. Adam office, design for a ceiling for the front drawing room at 15 Berkeley Square, 1769. SM Adam volume 11/213. Photograph: Ardon Bar-Hama

new ceilings in both drawing rooms as he is known to have designed friezes for the rooms. There is no extant design for the bedchamber ceiling and it is not known if a new interior decorative scheme was installed there. Nineteen Adam office drawings for 15 Berkeley Square survive at the Soane Museum. These include ceiling designs for the front drawing room, dating from 1769 and 1776 (Figs 54-55): the 1769 scheme was executed, and then redone to new Adam designs seven years later. The reason for this is unknown. The scheme of 1769 follows a typical Adam-style colourful design, while the 1776 scheme shows Adam's move towards delicacy in the 1770s, as well as utilising a colour scheme which hints at his Etruscan style. Adam also designed chimneypieces and gilt overmantel mirror frames for the two rooms.

Two months before Child died, his only offspring, Sarah, eloped with the roguish John Fane, 10th Earl of Westmorland, and therefore on his death Child vested his entire fortune in his widow, also Sarah. She was required to maintain Osterley and Upton Park, but 15 Berkeley Square was hers to do with as she pleased and she installed furniture by John Linnell and made improvements to the house in 1790 in preparation for her marriage a year later to Francis

Fig 55. Adam office, design for a ceiling for the front drawing room at 15 Berkeley Square, 1776. SM Adam volume 11/214. Photograph: Ardon Bar-Hama

Reynolds, 3rd Baron Ducie.[211] Following Lady Ducie's death in 1793, Child's estate – at his specific behest – was then placed in trust for his eldest granddaughter. This was an unusual course of action – clearly intended by Child to keep his fortune away from his son-in-law and the Earls of Westmorland – especially as the granddaughter, Lady Sarah Sophia Fane was not born until three years after Child had died.[212] Lord Ducie was granted the use of 15 Berkeley Square for his lifetime, but he chose not to live there, and instead it was occupied by Sarah Sophia's father, the Earl of Westmorland. In 1804, Sarah Sophia came of age, inherited the Child fortune – including 15 Berkeley Square – and married George Bussy Villiers, 5th Earl of Jersey.[213]

Sarah Sophia was a renowned hostess and undertook two schemes of improvements at 15 Berkeley Square to better suit this purpose, first to designs by Thomas Cundy in 1805,

[211] Ibid., p. 41.
[212] ODNB: Sarah Sophia Child-Villiers: http://www.oxforddnb.com/view/article/40795 (accessed 23/08/2016).
[213] Harris, 2000, p. 41.

and second to designs by Henry Crace in 1831. She continued to receive guests in the house every evening until her death in 1867 aged 81, when the Child property then passed into the possession of the Earls of Jersey.[214] The 7th Earl sold the lease of 15 Berkeley Square to the 5th Earl of Roseberry in 1888, who made alterations, including the amalgamation of Adam's front and back drawing rooms. When the house was sold again in 1939 it was demolished. There are no known photographs of the interiors prior to the demolition, although it is doubtful that anything of Adam's scheme survived, apart from fragments of the front drawing room ceiling which were sold and installed at Hinton Ampner, Hampshire.[215]

Lansdowne House

In 1761, John Stuart, 3rd Earl of Bute, acquired a large plot on the south side of Berkeley Square and commissioned Adam to make designs for a new house.[216] But instead of a terraced house, this was a detached urban palace (Fig. 56) – more like a country house that a town residence. Adam produced four different schemes before Bute and his adviser Thomas Worsley, Surveyor of the Office of Works, were satisfied.[217] Six drawings for Bute's house survive at the Soane Museum, although none of them show the final design. There are various plans for the house by Adam and others in the RIBA Drawings Collection, and further Adam drawings survive at Mount Stuart on the Isle of Bute, including designs for the façade and sections for the library which correspond with those in the Soane Museum collection.[218]

Bute was a scholar and statesman. He succeeded his father in 1723, and in 1736 he married Mary Wortley Montagu through whom he inherited the vast fortune of her parents, Edward and Lady Mary Wortley Montagu.[219] His involvement in public life was initially tentative. In 1737 he was elected as a Scottish representative peer but rarely appeared in the House of Lords, and in 1738 he was appointed as one of the commissioners of the police for Scotland. However, everything changed with the 1745 Jacobite uprising, which prompted Bute to relocate to London, where he became acquainted with Frederick, Prince of Wales, and was appointed as Lord of the Bedchamber to the Prince in 1750–51, Groom of the Stool in 1756 and tutor to the future King George III. Bute encouraged an 'isolationist foreign policy, the abolition of party distinctions, the purging of corruption, and the enhancement of the monarchical control over policy and patronage', causing some tension during the early years of George III's reign.[220]

As soon as George III succeeded to the throne in 1760, Bute joined the Privy Council, and a year later was made Secretary of State, as well as Ranger of Richmond Park in 1761 and a Knight of the Garter in 1762. But his sudden rise and his popularity with the King prompted jealousy and confusion, especially following William Pitt's resignation from the cabinet in 1761.

[214] Ibid., pp. 42-43.
[215] King, 2001, Volume 1, p. 311.
[216] Ibid., Volume 2, p. 128.
[217] Harris, 2001, pp. 113-14.
[218] RIBA Drawings Collection, J3/16/1–18, K12/3/1–5. F. Russell, 'The house that became a hostage', *Country Life*, 29 October 1998, p. 65.
[219] Russell, 1998, p. 65.
[220] ODNB: John Stuart, 3rd Earl of Bute: http://www.oxforddnb.com/view/article/26716?docPos=1 (accessed 23/08/2016).

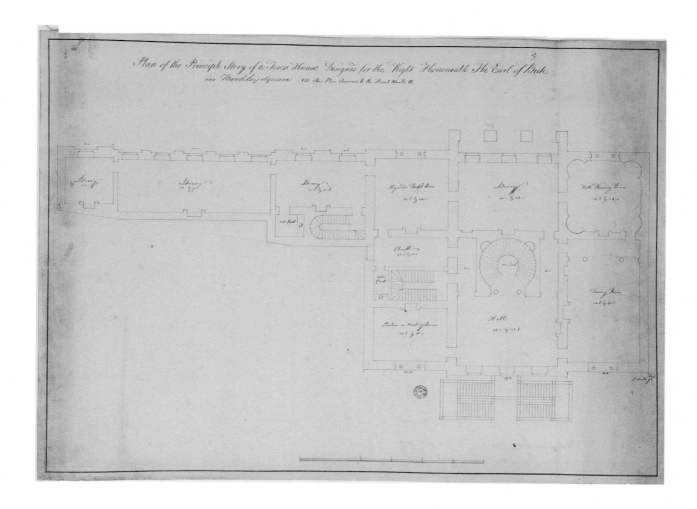

Fig 56. Adam office, plan showing one of four schemes for Bute House, Berkeley Square, *c.*1761–63. SM
Adam volume 39/49. Photograph: Ardon Bar-Hama

As a result, Bute suffered widespread attacks in the press, and when he served as First Lord of the Treasury from May 1762 to April 1763 – during which time he brought about peace with France – his political rivals continued to fan the flames of public hostility. This culminated in widespread unpopularity, with Bute being constantly lampooned, threatened and insulted in public: a situation which he found intolerable, and so resigned his position. The King, however, continued to seek Bute's advice causing further resentment, so Bute decided to retire to one of his county seats, Luton Park, Bedfordshire, which he had purchased in 1762.[221]

[221] Ibid.

Bute was not only a political figure but also a keen patron of artistic and intellectual activities. He was a Trustee of the British Museum in 1765–92 and President of the Society of Arts in 1780–92.[222] He was a renowned bibliophile and the Berkeley Square house was to include a 144-foot long library in a range to the rear of the house.[223] The central portion of the library design had a double-height rectangular space, flanked by octagonal domes, the whole encircled by a cantilevered gallery to give access to the upper shelves. Despite the scale of this library, Bute must have demanded yet more shelf space, as another smaller library was designed by Adam for the main body of the house.[224]

Having fled London, Bute no longer needed an urban palace, and he sold the unfinished house to the 2nd Earl of Shelburne in 1765. The terms of this sale were unusual. Bute was required to pay for the completion of the building to Adam's designs, while Shelburne's purchase payment of £22,000 (less than the cost to build the house) was deferred until 1773, with only £900 per annum in interest paid in the interim.[225]

William Petty, 2nd Earl of Shelburne was the eldest son of John Petty, 1st Earl of Shelburne. In 1765 he married Lady Sophia Carteret, daughter of John Carteret, 2nd Earl of Granville, and he married again in 1779, Lady Louise Fitzpatrick, daughter of John Fitzpatrick, 1st Earl of Upper Ossory. Shelburne was an army officer, attaining the rank of General in 1783, and also served as MP for Chipping Wycombe in 1760–61 until he succeeded his father and entered the House of Lords, where he served as First Lord of Trade in 1763, Secretary of State for the southern department in 1766–68, Secretary of State for Home Affairs in 1782, and following the death of Lord Rockingham he was First Lord of the Treasury for eight months in 1782–83. Much of Shelburne's time as First Minister was engaged in peace negotiations with America via the French and in 1784 he was rewarded for his public service and was created 1st Marquess of Lansdowne.[226]

Lansdowne had been one of Adam's earliest patrons, commissioning him to make alterations to his country seat of Bowood, Wiltshire in 1761. It is unsurprising therefore, that he should wish to continue with Adam's scheme for Bute's house on Berkeley Square – which would come to be known as Shelburne House and then as Lansdowne House. Alterations were made to the original scheme to suit Lansdowne's desires (Figs 57-58) and new designs for the interior decoration were commissioned from Adam in 1766. These include schemes for the entrance hall, drawing room, ante-room, dining room, library, stairwell, bedchamber, dressing room, gallery and many other spaces. The rooms were executed with chimneypieces by Benjamin and Thomas Carter, and painted panels by Gavin Hamilton, Giovanni Battista Cipriani and Antonio Zucchi; Cipriani's four panels for the ante-room were sold at Christie's in 1930.[227] Lady

[222] Ibid.
[223] King, 2001, Volume 2, p. 170.
[224] Ibid., p. 173.
[225] Russell, 1998, p. 67.
[226] ODNB: William Petty, 2nd Earl of Shelburne: http://www.oxforddnb.com/view/article/22070?docPos=2 (accessed 23/08/2016). HoP: William Petty, 2nd Earl of Shelburne: http://www.historyofparliamentonline.org/volume/1754-1790/member/petty-william-1737-1805 (accessed 23/08/2016).
[227] Stillman, 1966, p. 48. H. Potterton, 'A Neo-Classical Decorative Scheme: G.B. Cipriani at Lansdowne House', *Apollo*, October 1972, p. 332.

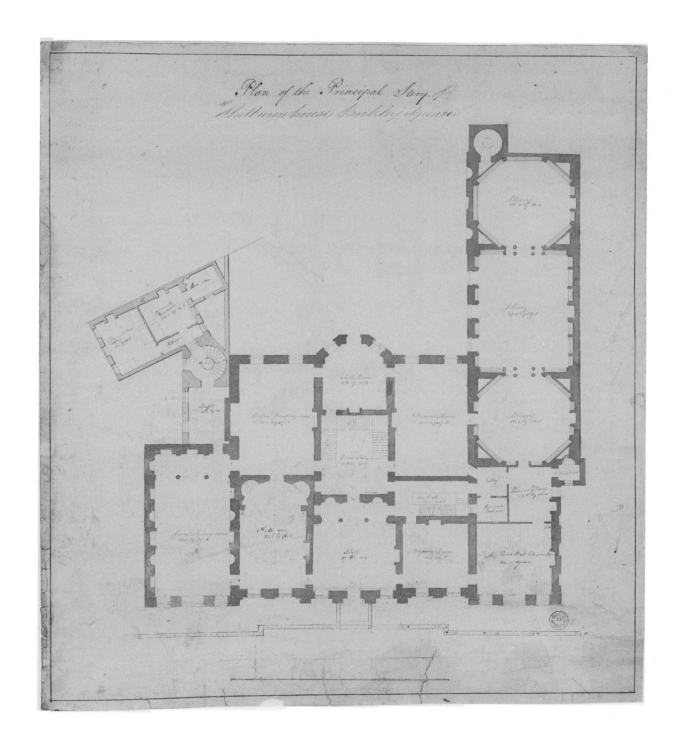

Fig 57. Adam office, plan for the ground floor of Lansdowne House, 1765. SM Adam volume 39/53.
Photograph: Ardon Bar-Hama

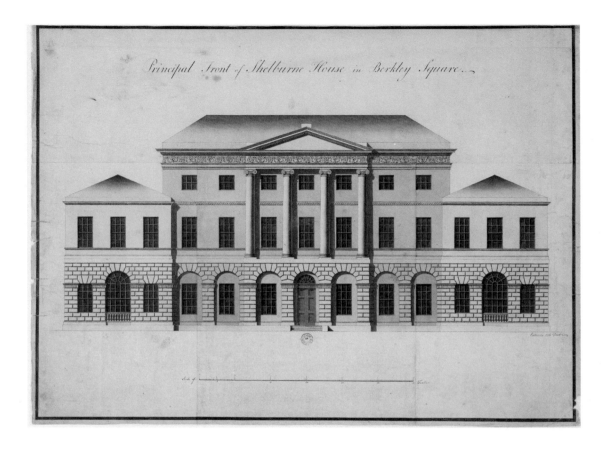

Fig 58. Adam office, design for the façade of Lansdowne House, 1765. SM Adam volume 39/50. Photograph: Ardon Bar-Hama

Shelburne recorded in her diary that she and her husband took up residence in the house in August 1768, despite some of the interiors still being unfinished.[228]

Perhaps Adam's finest designs for Lansdowne House were for the drawing room, variously conceived as an organ room for Bute, then a library, and finally executed as a drawing room with a Corinthian chimneypiece, Corinthian pilasters on the walls, and a tripartite ceiling with a large central medallion encircled by lunettes, and flanked by rows of lozenges (Fig. 59). The dining room, the largest single room in the house, was also an Adam tour de force, Antique in spirit with its monochromatic colour scheme, statues in niches and Spalatro order screen of columns. However, Adam's designs for a great library in the rear wing of the house were not executed, and despite the submission of alternative designs by Francesco Panini, Charles-Louis Clérisseau, François-Joseph Bélanger and Joseph Bonomi, Lansdowne prevaricated between a

---

[228] Harris, 2001, p. 116.

Fig 59. Adam office, design for a ceiling for the drawing room at Lansdowne House, 1767. SM Adam volume 11/83. Photograph: Ardon Bar-Hama

library and gallery space and after his death the room was completed as a library to designs by George Dance in 1786.[229] It was subsequently converted into a sculpture gallery by Sir Robert Smirke in 1816–19.[230]

By his death in 1805, Lansdowne's building projects had left him in debt and the entire contents of Lansdowne House were immediately sold.[231] However, the house itself remained in the possession of the Lords Lansdowne until the construction of Fitzmaurice Place, the link road between Berkeley Square and Curzon Street prompted the sale of the house in 1929, and its near-complete demolition in the early 1930s.[232] The remaining portion of Portland stone façade was partially reconstructed and a few rooms – much altered – were recast within the replacement building by Wimperis, Simpson and Guthrie, now the Lansdowne Club.[233]

[229] SM 68/5/1-6.
[230] King, 2001, Volume 2, p. 173.
[231] Harris, 2001, p. 113.
[232] King, 2001, Volume 1, p. 265.
[233] Weinreb, 2008, p 475.

The drawing room and dining room were removed prior to demolition and survive as period rooms installed at the Philadelphia Museum of Art and the Metropolitan Museum of Art, New York, respectively.[234]

Curzon Street

In 1715, a piece of land between Green Park and Hyde Park formerly known as Great Brookfield came into the possession of Sir Nathaniel Curzon of Kedleston Hall, Derbyshire.[235] Named after the freeholder, Curzon Street was developed piecemeal from the early 1720s, including a variety of houses and the famous Mayfair Chapel.[236]

30 Curzon Street

Originally two terraced houses, No. 30 Curzon Street was built in 1750–55 by an unknown architect.[237] Quickly joined together as one house, it now comprises four floors over a sunk basement, with a generous six-bay façade, rusticated on the ground floor, with alternating triangular and segmental pediments over the first-floor windows, and with a single-bay Doric porch off centre in the fifth bay. Soon after the two houses were joined the lease was acquired by the Hon. Henry Frederick Thynne who was the second son of Thomas, 2nd Viscount Weymouth by his second wife, Louisa Carteret, daughter of the 2nd Earl of Granville. He served as MP for Staffordshire in 1757–61 and Weobley in 1761–70, as well as clerk comptroller of the Board of Green Cloth in 1762–65, Master of the Household in 1768–70 and joint postmaster general in 1770–89. In 1776 Thynne succeeded to the estates of his maternal uncle, the 3rd Earl of Granville, took the name Carteret, and was created Baron Carteret in 1784. In 1810, at the age of 60, he married Eleanor Smart, his mistress of 43 years. The birth of their only son predated the marriage so Thynne was succeeded by his nephew.[238]

In 1771–73 Thynne commissioned Adam to redecorate the interior at 30 Curzon Street. His half-brother, the 3rd Viscount Weymouth was married to Lady Elizabeth Cavendish-Bentinck, the eldest daughter of the 2nd Duke of Portland, Adam's patron for the unexecuted designs for Portland House, New Cavendish Street in the early 1770s (see p. 47).[239] It was possibly through this connection that Thynne came to be acquainted with Adam. At 30 Curzon Street, Adam made designs for the interior, as well as for plate and furniture, and there are 18 surviving Adam office drawings for the scheme at the Soane Museum. Perhaps Adam's best contribution to the house was a magnificent segmentally vaulted drawing room, with ornamental plasterwork by Joseph Rose in the front room on the first floor of the house. Adam's drawings show a three-bay apsidal room, with three sculpture-filled niches in the apse, the segmentally vaulted ceiling had a fashionable Adam-style colour scheme in green and pink (Fig. 60).

[234] Harris, 2001, p. 113.
[235] Weinreb, 2008, p. 228.
[236] Bradley, 2003, p. 517.
[237] Ibid., p 519.
[238] HoP: Hon. Henry Frederick Thynne: http://www.historyofparliamentonline.org/volume/1754-1790/member/thynne-hon-henry-frederick-1735-1826 (accessed 16/08/2016).
[239] Bolton, 1922, Volume II, Index p. 36.

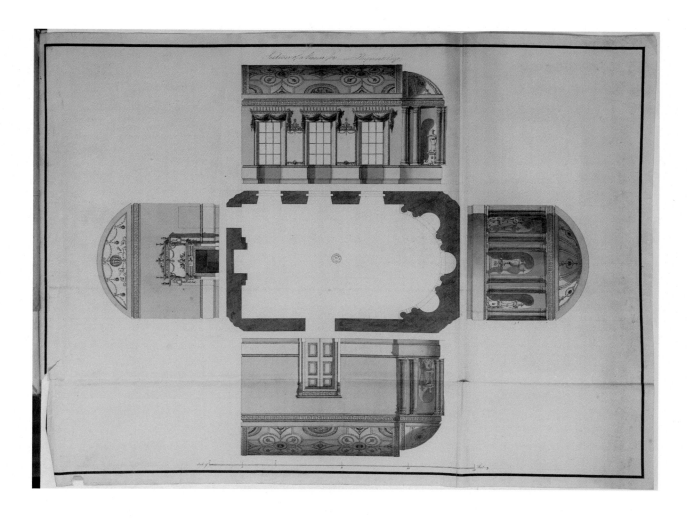

Fig 60. Adam office, design for the drawing room at 30 Curzon Street, 1771. SM Adam volume 50/73.
Photograph: Ardon Bar-Hama

Adam's drawing room survives without the original apsidal end, as does his entrance hall, and there are other twentieth-century Adam-revival interiors within the house.[240] 30 Curzon Street has been the location of the private members' gaming club Crockford's since 1983.[241]

Hertford Street

Hertford Street is an L-shaped street between Park Lane and Curzon Street, consisting of terraced houses dating from the 1760s when the street was laid out and developed for the

---

240 King, 2001, Volume 1, p. 307.
241 Bradley, 2003, p. 519.

landlord, Nathan Carrington.[242] It is thought to have taken its name from a nearby inn, the Hertford Arms, which no longer exists.[243] Once a fashionable domestic area, Hertford Street is now principally offices, but there is still a density of surviving Georgian buildings.

10 Hertford Street

Nos 8–13 Hertford Street, and possibly also Nos 17–22, were built in 1768–70 by Henry Holland and the carpenter John Elridge. No. 10, on the south side of the street, is larger than most and is composed of a five-storey, three-bay brick house with a stuccoed ground floor. Its first resident was General John Burgoyne who took the lease of the house in 1769.[244]

Burgoyne was the second son of Captain John Burgoyne and the grandson of Sir John Burgoyne, 3rd Baronet, of Sutton Park, Bedfordshire. He had little money of his own and relied on an income from his military career: he became lieutenant-colonel in 1758, major-general in 1762, and lieutenant-general in 1777 and moreover served as commander of the British forces in America from 1776, devising the plan to lead the British forces south from Canada, but eventually surrendering to the Americans at Saratoga in 1777. Burgoyne also served as MP for Midhurst in 1761–68 and Preston in 1768–92; as commander in chief in Ireland in 1782–84; and later in his life was also a playwright, his most famous works being inspired by his wife, and entitled 'The Heiress', and 'Maid of Oaks'.[245]

In 1743 Burgoyne eloped with Lady Charlotte Stanley, the youngest daughter of the 11th Earl of Derby, whom he had met through his friendship at school with Lord Strange, Charlotte's brother (and the 12th Earl of Derby's father – see 23 Grosvenor Square: p. 66). The Earl did not approve of the match and denied the couple Charlotte's dowry, causing them considerable financial difficulties and forcing them to flee to France in 1749 in a bid to avoid their creditors.[246] Their residence on the Continent afforded the Burgoynes the opportunity to befriend Adam during his Grand Tour (1754–58), before they returned to England in 1756 when the Earl finally relented and gave them £25,000.[247]

Having leased the house on Hertford Street from Holland in 1769, Burgoyne commissioned his friend Adam to design the interior.[248] The house is arranged as a typical terraced house, with a hall and stairwell to one side, and large rooms to front and rear. Fifteen of Adam's designs survive at the Soane Museum, and these include designs for neoclassical ceilings and chimneypieces for the front and rear drawing rooms on the first floor, including painted medallions by Antonio Zucchi, the ante-room adjacent to the front drawing room – above the entrance hall – and the dining room and parlour on the ground floor (Figs 61-62). Adam's interiors for Burgoyne were apparently admired, as his scheme for the front drawing room was reproduced for a Mrs Stevenson, also living on Hertford Street. Much of the interior was

---

[242] Ibid., p. 536.
[243] Weinreb, 2008, p. 395.
[244] Bradley, 2003, p. 536.
[245] HoP: John Burgoyne: http://www.historyofparliamentonline.org/volume/1754-1790/member/burgoyne-john-1723-92 (accessed 5/08/2016).
[246] HoP: John Burgoyne.
[247] J. Fleming, *Robert Adam and his circle*, 1962, p. 118. HoP: John Burgoyne.
[248] T. Draper, 'No 10 Hertford Street', *The Georgian Group Journal*, 1999, pp. 116–38.

Fig 61. Adam office, design for a ceiling for the front drawing room at 10 Hertford Street, 1769. SM Adam volume 13/145. Photograph: Ardon Bar-Hama

executed in accordance with Adam's designs, being completed in 1771, and largely survives *in situ*.

Following Lady Charlotte's death in 1776, Burgoyne remained at 10 Hertford Street, and from 1780 he took the actress Susan Cauldfield as his mistress and fathered four children.[249] On Burgoyne's death in 1792, the lease of 10 Hertford Street was acquired by Richard Brinsley Sheridan, the politician and dramatist, who lived there from 1795 to 1802; it has been known as Sheridan House ever since.[250] The building was used as offices between the Second World War and 1990 and was listed Grade I in 1958, but then unoccupied between 1990 and 1998 and was placed on the English Heritage 'Buildings at Risk' register.[251] Happily, it is now in private ownership and has been restored for domestic use, with Adam's ceilings renovated and

---

[249] HoP: John Burgoyne.
[250] Weinreb, 2008, p. 395.
[251] Historic England Listing: 10 Hertford Street: https://historicengland.org.uk/listing/the-list/list-entry/1230913 (accessed 5/08/2016).

Fig 62. Adam office, design for a chimneypiece for the front drawing room at 10 Hertford Street, 1769. SM Adam volume 22/268. Photograph: Ardon Bar-Hama

the chimneypieces from the front and back drawing rooms – stolen in 1996 – replaced with facsimiles based on Adam's designs at the Soane Museum.

Lock Hospital, Grosvenor Place

Grosvenor Place runs along the western boundary of Buckingham Palace Gardens. The first building here in 1747 was the Lock Hospital, founded for the care of women suffering from venereal disease.[252] At an unknown date Adam made designs for rebuilding the Lock Hospital and five drawings survive at the Soane Museum, which appear to date from the 1760s. These show a five-block building, with a large central domed and pedimented chapel, flanked by two-storey, five-bay curving links, and two-and-a-half storey, nine-bay wings presumably

[252] J. Bettley, 'Post Voluptatem Misericordia: The Rise and Fall of the London Lock Hospitals', *The London Journal*, Volume 10, 1984, issue 2, pp. 169–71.

Fig 63. Adam office, design for the façade of the Lock Hospital, *c*.1760–70. SM Adam volume 38/16. Photograph: Ardon Bar-Hama

containing hospital accommodation (Fig. 63). It is not known if Adam was commissioned to rebuild the Lock Hospital or if this was a speculative scheme. Indeed, it seems unlikely that a new building would have been commissioned as its foundation and construction had been relatively recent. Either way, Adam's designs were not executed. The hospital moved to a new site on Harrow Road in 1842 and the building on Grosvenor Place was demolished in 1846.[253]

Buckingham House

At the west end of the Mall, between St James's Park and Green Park, Buckingham House was built in 1702–5 by John Sheffield, 1st Duke of Buckingham at a cost of £8,000, to designs by William Winde, possibly in consultation with William Talman.[254] On the Duchess of Buckingham's death in 1742 the house passed to the Duke's illegitimate son Sir Charles Sheffield, who in 1760 approached the Treasury in the hope of renewing his lease of the land on which around half of the house stood. However, Sir Charles was unsuccessful and following negotiations, the house was purchased in 1762 by George III for £28,000.[255] It was intended to replace Somerset House as a dower house for Charlotte of Mecklenburg-Strelitz, whom the King had married the previous year, but the royal family began to use it as their private home, as it provided a more domestic atmosphere than the formality of the court at St James's Palace.[256]

During the 1760s–80s the house was adapted for use by the increasing royal family – 15 children in total – and the King's ever growing library.[257] This work was principally undertaken by Sir William Chambers, George III's former architecture tutor, who added large wings to

---

[253] Weinreb, 2008, p. 359.
[254] Bradley, 2003, p. 645.
[255] Colvin, 1976, p. 134.
[256] ODNB: Charlotte of Mecklenburg-Strelitz http://www.oxforddnb.com/view/article/5162?docPos=1 (accessed 4/08/2016).
[257] Colvin, 1976, p. 134.

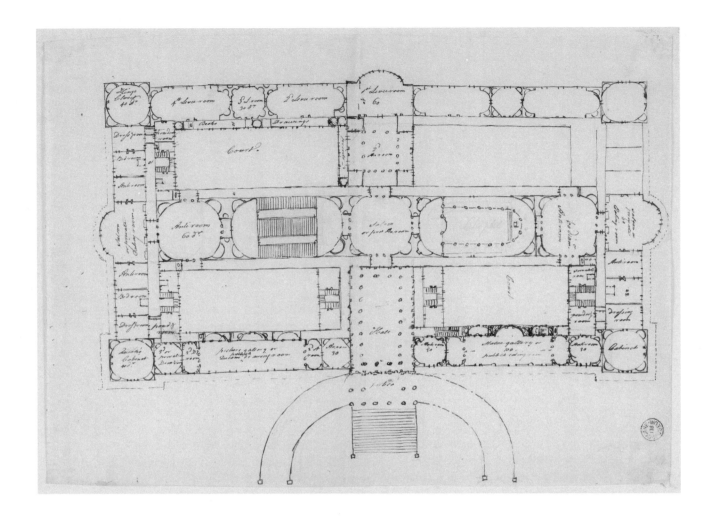

Fig 64. Robert Adam, design for alterations to Buckingham House, *c*.1761–63. SM Adam volume 4/138.
Photograph: Ardon Bar-Hama

either side.[258] Minor additions were also made by Adam in 1761–63. George III had met Adam in 1761, when he was appointed Architect to the King, jointly with Chambers. We know from Adam's obituary in the *Gentleman's Magazine* that he relinquished this position in 1768 when he was elected MP for Kinross, and was succeeded as Architect to the King by his brother James, who retained the position until its abolition in 1782.[259]

Although the fabric of Buckingham House was altered for George III by Chambers, Adam also made a proposal for this work in the early 1760s (Fig. 64). Six preliminary designs for a

258 Colvin, 2008, p. 244.
259 Ibid., pp. 41, 44.

quadrangular building in Adam's own hand are preserved at the Soane Museum and there is a finished drawing for the scheme in the collection at Hovingham Hall.[260] Adam proposed doubling the size of Buckingham's original house by extending the pavilions to each side and enclosing the courtyard by the addition of a fourth range. It has been noted that Adam's scheme for remodelling the principal (east) front of the house differed little from Chambers' executed design, suggesting that Chambers may have known of Adam's scheme before making his own.[261]

During the 1760s internal alterations were made to Buckingham House, when all of the doorcases and chimneypieces were replaced in the Queen's apartment and various new ceilings installed.[262] Adam was responsible for the chimneypiece in the saloon, the door between the staircase and the saloon (Fig. 65), and the ceiling in the Japanned room. Each made use

Fig 65. Adam office, design for a door between the stairwell and the saloon at Buckingham House, c.1762–63. SM Adam volume 49/7. Photograph: Ardon Bar-Hama

[260] Colvin, 1976, p. 137.
[261] A.A. Tait, *Robert Adam: Drawings and Imagination*, 1993, p. 52.
[262] Colvin, 1976, p. 136.

Fig 66. Adam office, design for an illumination for the garden at Buckingham House, 1763. SM Adam volume 49/1. Photograph: Ardon Bar-Hama

of his characteristic neoclassical style. Adam's chimneypiece in the saloon was removed to the Queen's Presence Chamber at Windsor Castle by William IV, but the rest of Adam's work was lost during alterations in the 1820s.[263] Adam's designs for these lost works survive at Windsor Castle, the RIBA drawings collection, and in the first volume of the *Works in architecture...* (1773–78), as well as among the drawings at the Soane Museum.[264] His design for the saloon doorcase at the Soane Museum beautifully exemplifies the new way in which the royal family was conducting itself, in a more domestic and private manner than had previously been the case at St James's Palace. This was not only a new door and doorcase in the fashionable Adam-style but an entirely new entrance created in a previously solid wall, allowing direct access from the staircase into the saloon, where previously it had been necessary to pass through the ante-room and the Japanned room. Adam's new door provided greater privacy for these other rooms of the suite, preventing them from being passages and allowing them to become the preserve of family life.[265]

Adam was also responsible for some more frivolous designs for Buckingham House, including a gilded clock bracket ornamented with royal insignia, though there is no evidence that this was executed. Other designs were commissioned from Adam by Queen Charlotte, firstly in 1763 for a magnificent illumination in the garden as a 25th birthday surprise for the King (Fig. 66), and then in 1780 for a pianoforte case.[266]

[263] King, 2001, Volume 1, p. 307.
[264] J. Harris (ed.), *Catalogue of the drawings collection of the Royal Institute of British Architects: A*, 1969, p. 16.
[265] Colvin, 1976, pp. 136-37.
[266] An account of George III's birthday celebration and Adam's illumination was given in the *Gentleman's Magazine*,

Apparently prompted by his sentiment for the family home, George III's son, George IV, applied to Parliament for the money to renovate Buckingham House.[267] The commission resulted in a large-scale remodelling, beginning in 1825, and completed at vast expense to designs by John Nash.[268] These works began the process of transforming Buckingham House into the 600-room palace that we know today. Buckingham Palace is – of course – the principal residence of the British sovereign, first lived in by Queen Victoria and currently the London home of Her Majesty Queen Elizabeth II.

Piccadilly

Piccadilly runs between Hyde Park Corner to the west and Piccadilly Circus to the east. Development of the street began in earnest from 1661, when the land along the eastern half of Piccadilly was granted to Henry Jermyn, 1st Earl of St Albans. At this time it was known as Portugal Street, in honour of Charles II's Portuguese Queen, Catherine of Braganza. The compliment to Catherine was quickly forgotten, however, as it was already known colloquially as Piccadilly, thanks to a house built in 1612 by a tailor, Robert Baker, at the east end – Baker had made his fortune selling fashionable collars known as 'picadils' at his shop in the Strand, and as a result of this, his home was known as Piccadilly Hall.[269] The only seventeenth-century survivals from the Earl of St Albans' development of Piccadilly are Burlington House and St James's Church (though the latter was heavily rebuilt following war damage); the rest of the street was redeveloped from the middle of the eighteenth century onwards.

Coventry House, 29 (later 106) Piccadilly

In the seventeenth century the eastern half of Piccadilly was largely composed of inns and shops facing Green Park. No. 29, on the corner of Brick Street, was built in 1759–62 on the former site of an inn called The Greyhound for Sir Henry Hunloke, 4th Baronet, of Wingerworth Hall, Derbyshire, to designs by an unknown architect, possibly Matthew Brettingham. Sir Henry had purchased a 99-year lease of the plot from William Pulteney, 1st Earl of Bath, who owned the surrounding estate; then in 1764 the remaining 94 years of the lease were transferred to George William, 6th Earl of Coventry, for 10,000 guineas.[270]

Coventry was the second son of the 5th Earl, succeeding his father in 1751.[271] He was considered a leader of fashion, most notably from his patronage of French decorative arts, including the Gobelins tapestries he purchased for his country house, Croome Court, Worcestershire.[272] In 1752 Coventry married his first wife, the famous Irish beauty Maria Gunning, by whom he had two children. His second wife was Barbara St John, the daughter of the 10th Lord St John of

June 1763, p. 30: 'A most magnificent temple and bridge, finely illuminated with about 4,000 glass lamps was erected in the garden. The painting on the front of the temple represented the King- giving peace to all parts of the earth...'
[267] Weinreb, 2008, pp. 108-9.
[268] Colvin, 2008, p. 732.
[269] Weinreb, 2008, p. 639.
[270] C. Gordon, *The Coventrys of Croome*, 2000, p. 133.
[271] Bolton, 1922, Volume II, Index p. 67.
[272] Hayward, 1980, Volume 1, p. 103.

Bletsoe. This second marriage brought Coventry a considerable amount of money, and in that same year he purchased 29 Piccadilly.[273] He was already in possession of townhouses in St James's and Grosvenor Squares, but it has been suggested by Catherine Gordon that the motivation to purchase a third townhouse was to provide Barbara with a London home unconnected with Coventry's first wife.[274] Indeed, this was not unique among Adam's patrons (see 20 St James's Square: p. 134). Replacing a country seat merely for a second wife's comfort would have been difficult, but providing a new townhouse was far more realistic.

On purchasing 29 Piccadilly, Coventry commissioned Adam to remodel the house. His choice of architect is unsurprising, as Adam was already working for Coventry at Croome Court. Alterations to the layout of the house were initially considered but never executed: there are seven preliminary sketches in Adam's hand for this work at the Soane Museum. Adam's interior designs, however, were executed and included redecoration in the ante-room and great room facing the street on the first floor; a third room behind the great room, which was redecorated as Lady Coventry's bedroom, and a small octagonal room beyond as Lady Coventry's dressing room (Fig. 67). Further to these interior decorative works, Adam also made improvements to the service quarters in the basement.[275]

Fig 67. Adam office, design for a ceiling for Lady Coventry's octagonal dressing room at Coventry House, 1765. SM Adam volume 14/85. Photograph: Ardon Bar-Hama

[273] Gordon, 2000, p. 102.
[274] Ibid., p. 133.
[275] Harris, 2001, chapter 3.

There are 56 surviving Adam drawings for Coventry House at the Soane Museum. These mostly show designs for interior decorative work, including ceilings, walls, chimneypieces, carpets, furniture, and even a set of sedan chair poles. The great room was the principal reception room of the house and Adam's ceiling design for it is particularly ornamental (Fig. 68). This and the neighbouring ante-room and bedroom was hung with red damask, so Adam's ceiling and furniture were his principal decorative contributions.[276] The ceiling was executed to a slightly revised version of Adam's drawings and with painted panels by Antonio Zucchi, all of which survive *in situ*. According to his bill, Adam charged Lord Coventry £20 for the ceiling design in June 1765; one month later working drawings were provided at a cost of five guineas, enabling construction to begin; in November 1765 a drawing showing alterations to the original design was produced for a guinea.[277]

Shortly after his father's death, the 7th Earl of Coventry commissioned repairs to the house in 1810–11, as well as a cast-iron balcony for the principal front, and the raising of the top floor, all to designs by Thomas Cundy.[278] Apart from Cundy's early nineteenth-

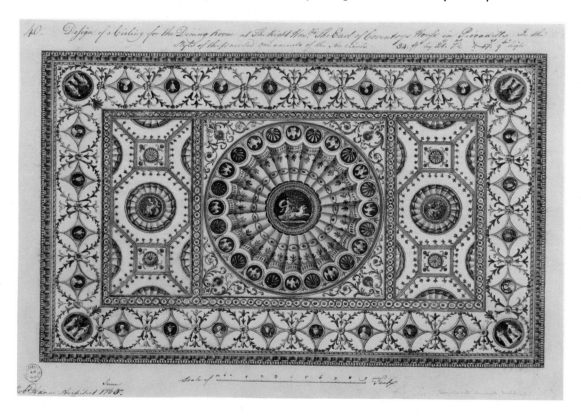

Fig 68. Adam office, design for a ceiling for the great room at Coventry House, 1765. SM Adam volume 11/40. Photograph: Ardon Bar-Hama

[276] Ibid., p. 13.
[277] Ibid., pp. 55-56.
[278] Colvin, 2008, p. 292.

Fig 69. Coventry House, 2016. Photograph: Lewis Bush

century work, the original façade survives (Fig. 69). The house remained the principal London residence of the Earls of Coventry until 1848. Twenty years later it was purchased by George Warren, Baron de Tabley, for use by the St James' Club (of which he was a Trustee), and the club was to remain here for over a century, until it merged with Brooks' Club in 1978.[279] During the St James' Club's tenure various alterations were made, including the demolition of the stables to accommodate a rear extension containing gaming rooms.[280] Now renumbered as 106, the house was until recently used by International House, a language school, but in 2007 a short lease was acquired by the London campus of Limkokwing University. The lease is currently for sale again and the building's future is uncertain.

147 Piccadilly

The central portion of St Albans' development on Piccadilly – between Swallow Street and Stratton Street – was the location of various large townhouses, including No. 147, later the residence of Henry Fox, 1st Baron Holland, the second son of a wealthy financier, Sir Stephen Fox. Following a political career serving as MP for Hindon in 1735–41; New Windsor in 1741–61 and Dunwich in 1761–63, Fox was created Lord Holland, Baron Foxley in April 1763. Holland was also Surveyor General in 1737–43, Lord of the Treasury in 1743–46, Secretary of the War Office in 1746–55, Secretary of State for the southern department in 1755–56, and Paymaster General in 1757–65. These various public offices – particularly that of Paymaster General – were extremely lucrative, and allowed Holland to undertake costly building projects during his retirement.[281]

In 1763 – the year he was elevated to his Barony – Holland purchased No. 147 Piccadilly for £16,000.[282] Being a century old, the house did not meet Holland's expectations and a year later Adam was commissioned to produce designs for rebuilding. Adam's plans for the house itself do not survive, but the commission included a handsome screen wall and gate across the front of the property (Fig. 70), for which there are two drawings at the Soane Museum. (There is an alternative preliminary design at the Victoria and Albert Museum.)[283] Adam's design shows a five-bay screen wall. Its central pedimented carriage arch is articulated by engaged Spalatro order columns and flanked by links ornamented with urn-filled niches and relief panels containing swags. Beyond are lodges with pyramidal roofs and doors surmounted by Diocletian fanlights.

However, at the time of Adam's designs, Holland's political career was nearing an end, and with it his time in London. As a result, none of Adam's proposals for 147 Piccadilly were ever carried out and instead Holland concentrated his efforts on building a country house, Holland House (later Kingsgate Castle), in Kent.[284] This was built on the cliffs above Kingsgate Bay around

[279] T. Murdoch, 'A mirror designed by Robert Adam: an Adam mirror for Coventry House returns to London', *National Art Collections Fund Annual Report*, 1992, p. 46.
[280] Bradley, 2003, p. 564.
[281] ODNB: Henry Fox, 1st Baron Holland: http://www.oxforddnb.com/view/article/10033?docPos=1 (accessed 28/07/2016). HoP: Henry Fox, 1st Baron Holland: http://www.historyofparliamentonline.org/volume/1715-1754/member/fox-henry-1705-74 (accessed 27/07/2016).
[282] SoL, Volume XXXII, 1963, p. 369.
[283] A. Rowan, *Catalogues of architectural drawings in the Victoria and Albert Museum: Robert Adam*, 1988, p. 60.
[284] ODNB: Henry Fox, 1st Baron Holland.

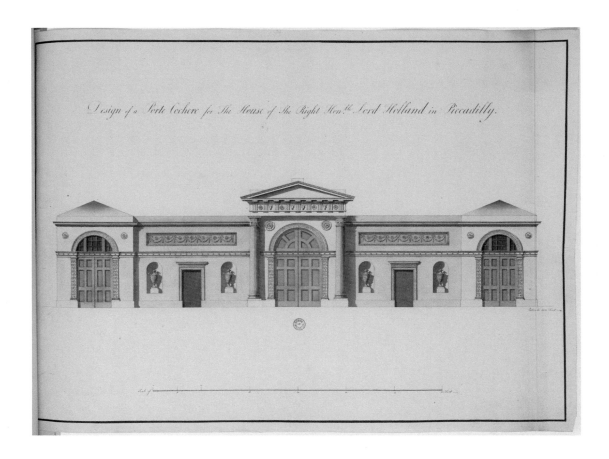

Fig 70. Adam office, design for a screen wall and gateway at 147 Piccadilly, 1764. SM Adam volume 51/68. Photograph: Ardon Bar-Hama

1762–68 to designs by Thomas Wynne, 1st Baron Newborough.[285] A single surviving design at the Soane Museum, for the ceiling of Lady Holland's bedroom, shows that Adam had been approached for at least one interior scheme for the house in Kent in 1767 but it was not executed.

As Holland's retirement was spent largely in Kent, he quickly lost interest in 147 Piccadilly. His desire to return to Kent is apparent from a letter he wrote to Horace Walpole on 14 August 1767: 'I beg you to write, however late, to my house in Piccadilly tomorrow night… You know my going to Kingsgate or not depends on what you tell me.'[286] He sold 147 Piccadilly in 1771, after only eight years of ownership, to Sir Peniston Lamb for £16,500.[287] Sir Peniston, who was created 1st Viscount Melbourne in 1772, immediately rebuilt the house to designs by Sir

285 Colvin, 2008, p. 1203.
286 Yale Edition, *Horace Walpole's Correspondence*, Volume 30, p. 247: http://images.library.yale.edu/hwcorrespondence/page.asp (accessed 28/07/2016).
287 Rowan, 1988, p. 60.

William Chambers: Melbourne House – as it was then known – was completed in 1774. It was sold in 1802 to Alexander Copland, a developer, who commissioned designs from Henry Holland to convert the building into apartments for bachelors, and by these means the building now known as Albany was created.[288]

Piccadilly at Hyde Park Corner, designs for Lord Shelburne

William Petty, 2nd Earl of Shelburne, later 1st Marquis of Lansdowne, had been Adam's patron at Bowood, and would become his patron at Lansdowne House on Berkeley Square (see p. 78).

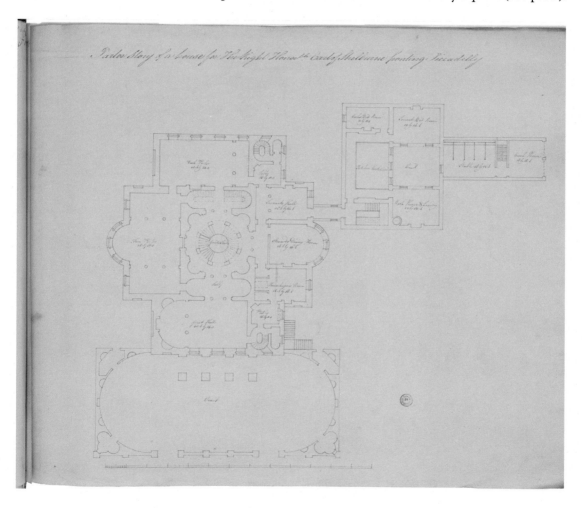

Fig 71. Adam office, plan for the ground floor of a house at Hyde Park Corner for Lord Shelburne, 1761. SM Adam volume 43/89. Photograph: Ardon Bar-Hama

[288] SoL, Volume XXXII, 1963, p. 369.

Fig 72. Adam office, design for the façade of a house at Hyde Park Corner for Lord Shelburne, 1761. SM Adam volume 43/87. Photograph: Ardon Bar-Hama

On succeeding his father in 1761, Shelburne acquired a plot of land at the west end of Piccadilly at Hyde Park Corner with the intention of building himself a townhouse.[289] Presumably this was motivated by the numerous public activities regularly bringing him to London. For this scheme too, Adam was commissioned to make designs and nine extant drawings at the Soane Museum show a generous three-storey, seven-bay Greek cross-shaped house, with an elliptical court at the front

[289] King, 2001, Volume 2, p. 130.

and a service wing to the rear (Figs 71-72). Shelburne sent Adam's plan to General Robert Clerk in Paris for comment; he thought it 'admirable … according to the situation circumstances & extent of the building', but said he could not understand how the Shelburnes could possibly make do with 'only one floor'.[290] The house was not executed and instead in 1765 Shelburne purchased the shell of Adam's house built for Lord Bute on Berkeley Square which would become Lansdowne House.

Piccadilly at Hyde Park Corner, designs for Lord Barrymore

In 1790 a plot at the western end of Piccadilly at Hyde Park Corner was purchased by Richard Barry, 7th Earl of Barrymore.[291] By the age of eleven, Barrymore had lost both parents, and perhaps as a consequence became rather eccentric. He spent lavishly on building works, including £60,000 on a private theatre at Wargrave, Berkshire, which was demolished and its contents sold in 1792 in order to pay Barrymore's debts. Being a member of the Irish peerage, Barrymore was able to serve as an MP for Haytesbury in 1791–93, although this was only done in an attempt to avoid his Irish creditors. In 1792 – the same year that he was declared bankrupt – Barrymore eloped to Gretna Green with Charlotte Goulding, the daughter of a sedan chairman. Barrymore had joined the Berkshire militia in 1789, and was promoted to Captain in 1793, only to die shortly afterwards when he accidentally shot himself. He was only 24.[292]

Having been in need of a London home to help him pursue a political career, Barrymore commissioned Adam to make designs for a 32 by 85 foot terraced house for a plot at the west end of Piccadilly (Fig. 73).[293] Five drawings for Barrymore's house survive at the Soane Museum, showing a relatively modest four-storey, three-bay terraced house, with a central pedimented front door to the ground floor and ironwork balconettes to the upper-floor windows. Plans for the basement, ground, first and second floors show an interior arranged with Adam's characteristic variety of circular, oval and apsidal rooms (Figs 74-75). It is interesting to note a discrepancy between the ground-floor plan and elevation: one has a carriage arch, the other a large entrance hall spanning the full width of the house.

Hastily applied annotations to Adam's plans show minor alterations to the design and one on the second-floor plan reads: *bed chamber / my*, suggesting that it was Barrymore himself who made these annotations. Another inscription in the Adam office draughtsman's hand reads: *Lady Barrymore's Bed Chamber*. The Lady Barrymore in question cannot refer to Lord Barrymore's mother, who had died a decade earlier, and he did not elope with Charlotte Goulding until two years after the drawings are thought to have been made. Perhaps when Barrymore commissioned Adam he was speculating on an imminent marriage, with no idea that he would soon be bankrupt or that his life would be so tragically cut short. Adam's scheme was never realised, most likely owing to Barrymore's financial difficulties, and he sold the plot in May 1792 around the time of his bankruptcy.[294]

[290] BL, Add MS 88906/01/010, ff. 19–20, 29–30, 32–3.
[291] King, 2001, Volume 2, p. 130.
[292] HoP: 7th Earl of Barrymore: http://www.historyofparliamentonline.org/volume/1790-1820/member/barry-richard-1769-93 (accessed 11/08/2016).
[293] King, 2001, Volume 2, p. 130.
[294] Bolton, 1922, Volume II, Index p. 110.

Fig 73. Adam office, design for the façade of a house at Hyde Park Corner for Lord Barrymore, *c*.1790. SM
Adam volume 32/106. Photograph: Ardon Bar-Hama

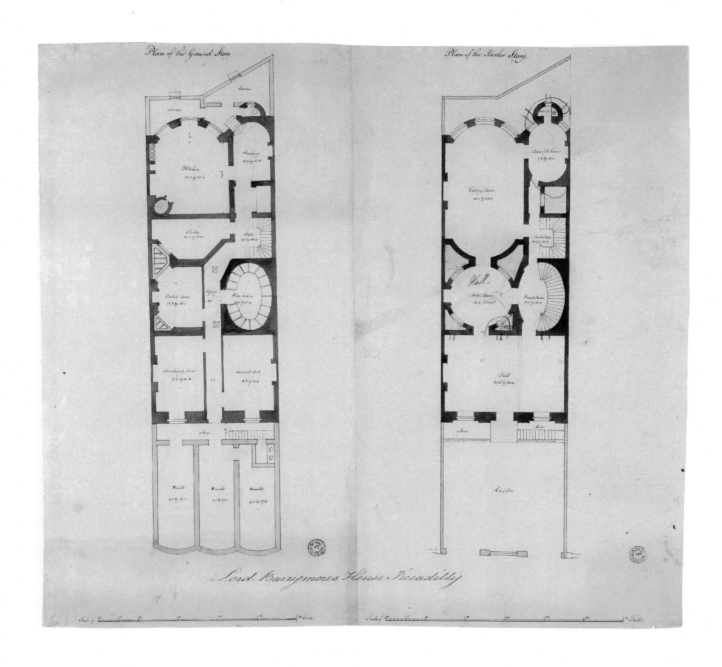

Fig 74. Adam office, plan of the basement and ground floors of a house at Hyde Park Corner for Lord Barrymore, *c*.1790. SM Adam volume 32/107-8. Photograph: Ardon Bar-Hama

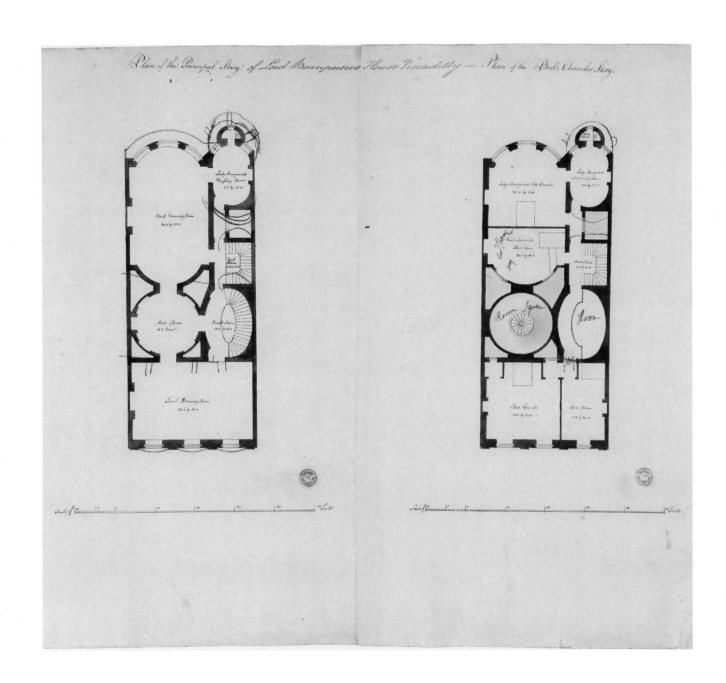

Fig 75. Adam office, plan of the first and second floors of a house at Hyde Park Corner for Lord Barrymore, *c.*1790. SM Adam volume 32/109-10. Photograph: Ardon Bar-Hama

Apsley House

Apsley House has the memorable address of 'No. 1, London', and is found at the west end of Piccadilly at Hyde Park Corner. It was built in 1772–78 by the Hon. Henry Bathurst to designs by Adam.[295] Bathurst was the second son of Allen Bathurst, 1st Earl Bathurst, and his maternal grandfather was Sir Peter Apsley of Apsley, Sussex. Embarking on a career as a lawyer in 1736, he joined Lincoln's Inn in 1743 and was appointed King's Counsel in 1746. Bathurst also served as MP for Cirencester in 1735–54, solicitor general to the Prince of Wales in 1745–48, attorney general to Frederick, Prince of Wales and George, Prince of Wales in 1748–54, justice of the common pleas in 1754–71, commander of the great seal in 1770–71, Lord Chancellor in 1771–78, and Lord President of the Council in 1779–82. In 1771 Bathurst was rewarded for his public service when he was created Baron Apsley, and in 1775 he succeeded his father as 2nd Earl Bathurst.[296]

Adam's house was smaller than Apsley House is now. Its original appearance is beautifully recorded on two Meissen plates of *c.*1818 belonging to the Victoria & Albert Museum.[297] It was a three-storey, five-bay plain brick block, with a Corinthian porch on the principal (south) front (Fig. 76-77), and was originally an end-of-terrace house until its neighbour, the penultimate house on Piccadilly, was demolished in order to extend Park Lane. This left Apsley House detached from Piccadilly and with an east front of blind windows. Surviving drawings for the house at the Soane Museum show the expected facilities: service rooms and cellars in the basement, an entrance hall, dining room, library and parlour on the ground floor as well as a small octagonal dressing room, and three drawing rooms and an apartment on the first floor, with each floor connected by an elegant elliptical staircase or an oval back stair. Eileen Harris has noted the imperfection of Adam's layout at Apsley House, particularly on the first floor, as it did not allow a complete circuit of the reception rooms as at various other Adam townhouses, such as Lansdowne House and 20 St James's Square.[298]

The original interiors were designed by Adam in 1774–75 and the drawings include ceilings, chimneypieces and wall treatments. Interesting features include what is probably Adam's first use of the Etruscan style of interior decoration in the circular dressing room, with a black and terracotta colour scheme (Fig. 78), and the chimneypiece for the dining room, which Eileen Harris has noted is similar to one designed by Giovanni Battista Piranesi for Burghley House and which he published in 1769 in his *Diverse maniere d'adornare i cammini* (Fig. 79).[299] Adam's 1778–79 designs for furniture at Apsley House include seat furniture for various rooms, door furniture, tripods, a clock case, a commode (possibly executed by Ince and Mayhew), pier tables, and eleven gilded mirrors and girandoles: those executed can be attributed to Sefferin Nelson.[300]

---

[295] Colvin, 2008, p. 49.
[296] ODNB: Henry Bathurst: http://www.oxforddnb.com/view/article/1694?docPos=1 (accessed 17/08/2016). HoP: Hon. Henry Bathurst: http://www.historyofparliamentonline.org/volume/1715-1754/member/bathurst-hon-henry-1714-94 (accessed 17/08/2016).
[297] King, 2001, Volume 1, p. 280.
[298] E. Harris, 'Adam at No. 1 London', *Country Life*, 1 November 2001, p. 99.
[299] Harris, *Country Life*, 2001, p. 101.
[300] Ibid., p. 100.

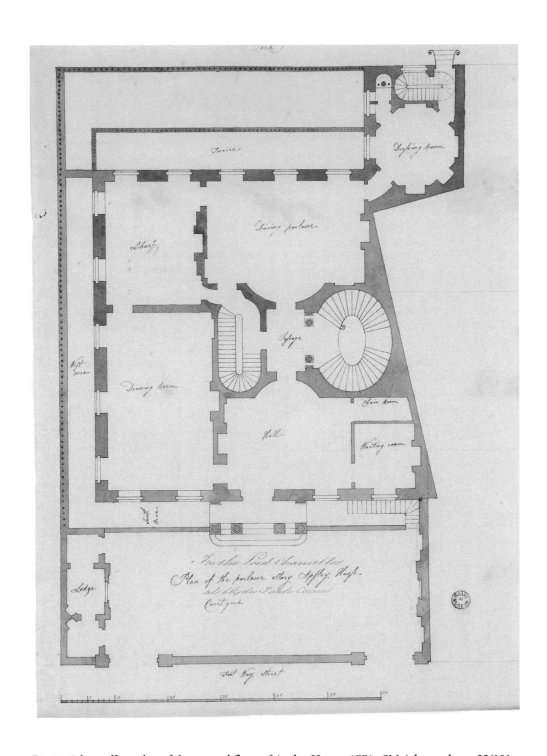

Fig 76. Adam office, plan of the ground floor of Apsley House, 1771. SM Adam volume 32/101.
Photograph: Ardon Bar-Hama

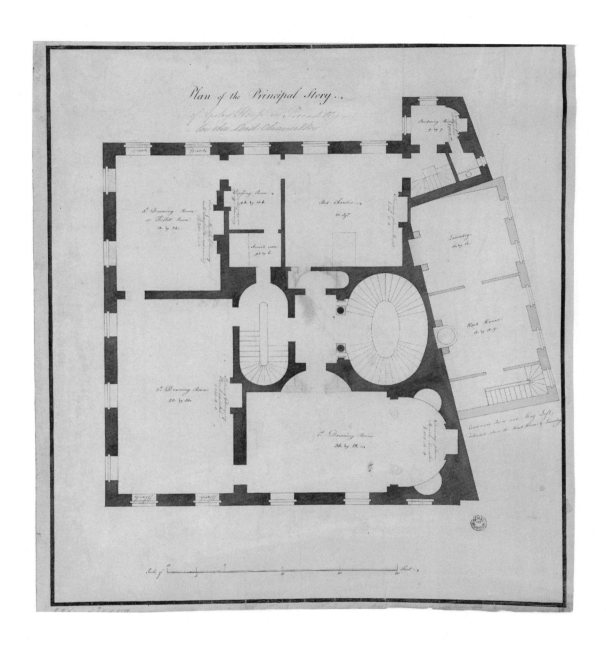

Fig 77. Adam office, plan of the first floor of Apsley House, 1771. SM Adam volume 32/102. Photograph: Ardon Bar-Hama

In 1807 Richard, 1st Marquess of Wellesley, Wellington's brother, acquired Apsley House for £16,000 from the 3rd Earl Bathurst. When the Duke of Wellington returned from war he paid his brother £40,000 for the house in 1817.[301] The Duke commissioned Benjamin and Philip

---

[301] J. Stourton, *Great houses of London*, 2012, p. 135.

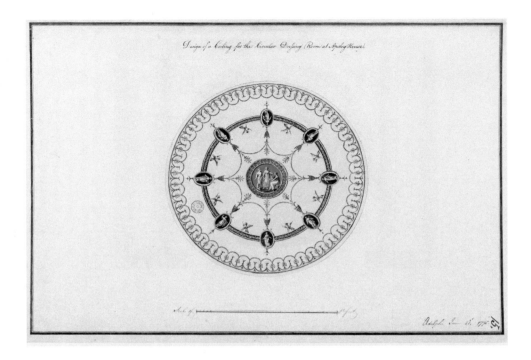

Fig 78. Adam office, design for a domed ceiling for the octagonal dressing room at Apsley House, 1775. SM Adam volume 14/15. Photograph: Ardon Bar-Hama

Wyatt to make alterations and additions, including an extra two bays, a new frontage of Bath stone and the addition of a giant Corinthian portico.[302] Only fragments of Adam's work survive, including the chimneypieces in the library (now the private dining room) and the dining parlour (now the library) on the ground floor; and on the first floor, the chimneypiece and frieze in the first drawing room (now the Piccadilly drawing room); the ceiling, chimneypiece and frieze in the second drawing room (now the portico room); and the chimneypiece in the third drawing room (now the yellow drawing room).[303] On the 1st Duke's death in 1852 the house became his memorial and was opened to the public, being gifted to the British nation in 1947 by the 7th Duke.[304] The Wellington Museum opened there in 1952, and Apsley House came into the guardianship of English Heritage in 2004.[305]

[302] Colvin, 2008, p. 1173: Bradley, 2003, p. 485.
[303] R. Lea, 'The Robert Adam drawings for the building and furnishing of Apsley House 1771-9', *Historic properties presentation*, English Heritage, September 2005, pp. 14-15.
[304] Stourton, 2012, p. 141.
[305] Weinreb, 2008, p. 24.

Fig 79. Adam office, design for a chimneypiece for the dining room at Apsley House, 1774. SM Adam volume 23/59. Photograph: Ardon Bar-Hama

Deputy Ranger's Lodge, Green Park

Probably enclosed by Henry VIII, Green Park comprises a 51-acre triangular plot between Piccadilly and Constitution Hill, and is so-called owing to its lush vegetation.[306] On the park's northern boundary along Piccadilly, between Old Park Lane and Down Street on the opposite side of the road, Adam built a modest villa known as the Deputy Ranger's Lodge.[307] This was designed in 1766 for Colonel the Hon. Archibald Montgomerie, who – as well as being an army officer and MP for Ayrshire in 1761–68 – was Deputy Ranger of Hyde Park and St James's Park in 1766–68. He succeeded his older brother as 11th Earl of Eglington in 1769 and became a Scottish Representative Peer.[308]

Adam's designs are thought to have been executed in accordance with his drawings (Figs 80-81).[309] The surviving drawings at the Soane Museum show a two-storey, five-bay building with a three-bay bow to the rear, and the central three bays at the front slightly projecting and surmounted by a pediment. Inside Adam provided service rooms flanking an entrance hall and octagonal parlour or eating room, and above are two apartments – comprising a bedchamber and dressing room – flanking an octagonal drawing room. There are no surviving Adam office interior decorative schemes for this modest but well-designed house, which was demolished in 1842.[310]

---

[306] Bradley, 2003, p. 656: Weinreb, 2008, pp. 350-51.
[307] King, 2001, Volume 1, p. 267.
[308] HoP: Hon. Archibald Montgomerie: http://www.historyofparliamentonline.org/volume/1754-1790/member/montgomerie-hon-archibald-1726-96 (accessed 22/08/2016).
[309] King, 2001, Volume 1, p. 267.
[310] Bradley, 2003, p. 657.

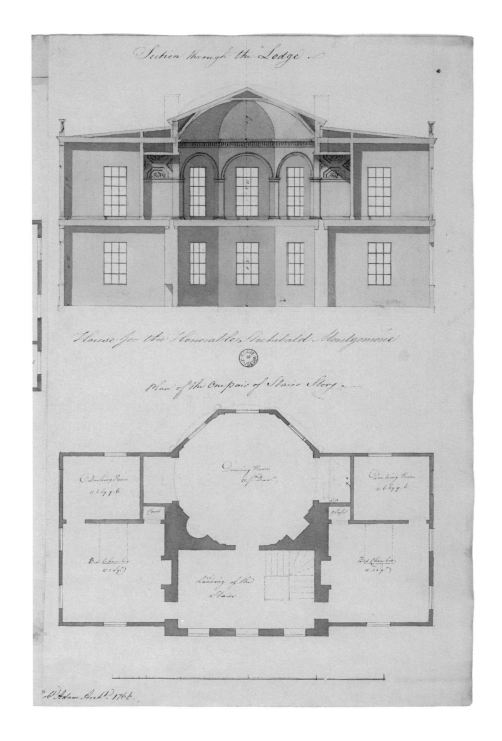

Fig 80. Adam office, plan and section of the Deputy Ranger's Lodge, Green Park, 1766.
SM Adam volume 42/28. Photograph: Ardon Bar-Hama

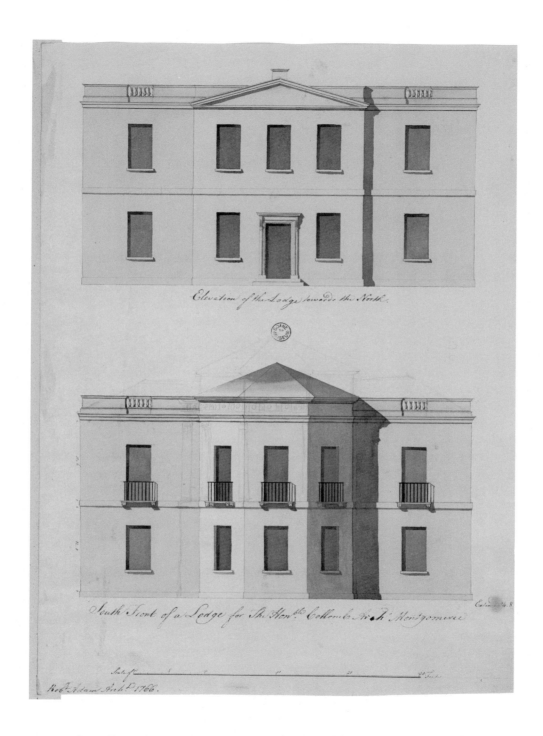

Elevation of the Lodge towards the North.

South Front of a Lodge for The Hon.ble Colloms Arch. Montgomerie

Rob.t Adam Arch.t 1766.

Fig 81. Adam office, design showing the front and rear elevations of the Deputy Ranger's Lodge, Green Park, 1766. SM Adam volume 42/26. Photograph: Ardon Bar-Hama

Arlington Street

Arlington Street is a cul-de-sac, off Piccadilly, and located between Green Park and St James's Square. It was developed by a Mr Pym in the late 1680s on land (formerly part of Green Park) which had been granted to Henry Bennet, 1st Earl of Arlington, by Charles II in 1681. During the eighteenth century it was home to many significant figures, including Robert and Horace Walpole, Lady Mary Wortley Montagu, Lord North, William Pulteney and Lord and Lady Nelson.[311] In 1768 Horace Walpole wrote: 'from the earliest memory Arlington Street has been the ministerial street', such was its popularity with members of government.[312]

19 Arlington Street

No. 19, situated on the west side of Arlington Street at its south end, was rebuilt by an unknown architect for Lord Carteret, 2nd Earl of Granville in 1732–38.[313] It was purchased for £15,000 in 1763 by Sir Lawrence Dundas, the second son of Thomas Dundas of Fingask, a moderately successful draper.[314] Dundas began his career at his father's shop, later becoming a wine merchant, but subsequently amassed a fortune working as Commissary-General and contractor of the army during the Seven Years' War. His great wealth earned Dundas the moniker 'nabob of the north', enabling him to purchase estates all over England, Scotland and Ireland and to forge a political career by buying his way into the Whig elite. He served as MP for Linlithgow Burghs in 1747–48, Newcastle-under-Lyme in 1762–68, Edinburgh in 1768–80 and 1781 and Richmond in 1780–81. Moreover, he was a governor of the Royal Bank of Scotland in 1764–77 and managed to negotiate a baronetcy in 1762.[315]

At both his country estate of Moor Park, Hertfordshire, and his London townhouse at 19 Arlington Street, Sir Lawrence employed Adam to make improvements during the period 1763–66. Adam made designs for an additional wing at the rear of the townhouse, with a three-bay canted bow facing Green Park, and containing a new great room. Survey drawings were made in 1763 enabling Adam to make designs for the extension and these are the only surviving graphic record of the building prior to its demolition (Figs 82-83). It was composed as a typical terraced house, arranged over three floors above a basement, but set back from the road behind a porter's lodge and courtyard. Nothing came of Adam's plans for structural alterations and a simplified extension was added at a later date.[316] However, Adam's designs for the interior were executed: he hung the walls with red damask, and collaborated with Thomas Chippendale to provide furniture.[317] Adam's work in the gallery of the staircase

---

[311] Weinreb, 2008, p. 26.
[312] Bradley, 2003, p. 602.
[313] J. Harris, 'The Dundas Empire', *Apollo* 86, September 1967, p. 177.
[314] Harris, 2007, p. 143.
[315] ODNB: Dundas family: http://www.oxforddnb.com/view/article/64103/64107 (accessed 27/07/2016). HoP: Sir Lawrence Dundas: http://www.historyofparliamentonline.org/volume/1754-1790/member/dundas-sir-lawrence-1710-81 (accessed 27/07/2016).
[316] King, 2001, volume 1, p. 307.
[317] Harris, 2007, p. 143.

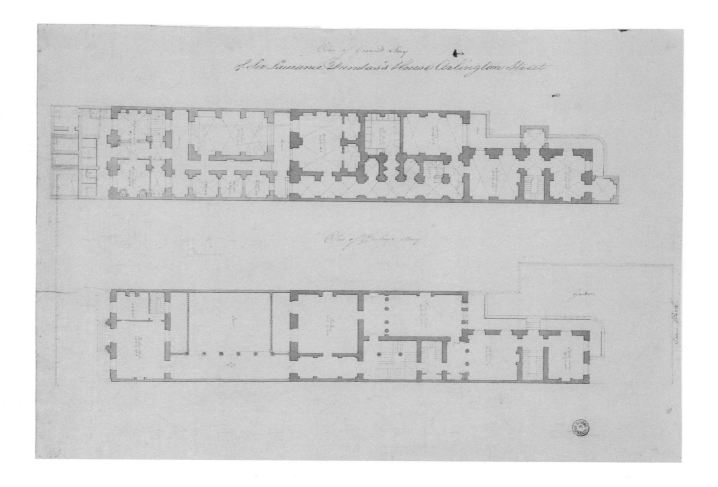

Fig 82. Adam office, survey drawing showing plans of 19 Arlington Street, 1763. SM Adam volume 32/52. Photograph: Ardon Bar-Hama

survived until as late as 1921 when *Country Life* magazine undertook a photographic survey of the house.[318]

Eleven drawings from the Adam office for 19 Arlington Street survive at the Soane Museum. These include the survey drawings of the house made in 1763, Adam's unexecuted designs for the rear extension and various designs for furniture, including a tripod table and pier glasses for the gallery, both of 1765, executed in accordance with Adam's designs and sold at Sotheby's

---

[318] *Country Life Picture Library*: www.countrylifeimages.co.uk (accessed 27/07/2016).

Elevation of an Addition proposed to be made to Sir Lawrence Dundas Baronet The House in Arlington Street Fronting the Green park

Fig 83. Adam office, design for a rear extension at 19 Arlington Street, *c.*1763–65. SM Adam volume 32/50.
Photograph: Ardon Bar-Hama

Fig 84. Adam office, design for a sofa for the saloon at 19 Arlington Street, 1764. SM Adam volume 17/74. Photograph: Ardon Bar-Hama

in 1934.[319] There is also a beautiful design for a sofa made for the saloon in 1764. Previously a dining room, the saloon was located on the first floor at the front of the house. Two sofas were made to Adam's design – along with four en suite armchairs – by Chippendale.[320] Adam's interior in the saloon was lost in 1784 when it was hung with the Gobelins Boucher-Neilson tapestries from the gallery at Moor Park, along with a matching suite of furniture; to make room for this the original furniture was moved to the corresponding room on the floor below. The sofas and armchairs for the saloon at 19 Arlington Street are thought to have been the most expensive ever made in this style (Fig. 84).[321] They were sold by the Marquis of Zetland at Sotheby's in 1947, and then again at Christie's in 1997, and are now dispersed between Duff House, Banff, the National Museum of Scotland, Edinburgh and the Victoria and Albert Museum, London.[322]

Following Sir Lawrence's death, Moor Park was sold by his son Thomas in 1784. The contents were moved to 19 Arlington Street and Aske Hall, Yorkshire.[323] 19 Arlington Street

[319] Harris, 2007, p. 144.
[320] Beard, 1978, p. 66.
[321] Harris, 2007, p. 143.
[322] E. Harris, *The furniture of Robert Adam*, 1963, p. 91. Christie's, *Dundas Masterpieces. The Property of the Marquess of Zetland and the 3rd Marquess of Zetland's Will Trust*, 3 July 1997, pp. 26-34.
[323] Harris, 1967, pp. 176-77.

remained the townhouse of the Dundas family – by then elevated as Marquises of Zetland – until its sale in 1934, followed by its demolition in 1936. Nos 17-20 Arlington Street were rebuilt in the same year to designs by Michael Rosenauer and now form Arlington House, a block of mansion flats.[324]

23 Arlington Street

The original seventeenth-century townhouse numbered 23 in Arlington Street is thought to have been rebuilt along with most of the other houses in the street in the 1730s, to the designs of an unknown architect.[325] In the mid-eighteenth century it was the townhouse of Sir George Colebrooke.

George Colebrooke was the third son of James Colebrooke, a London banker originally from Arundel, who in 1761 succeeded his brother James as 2nd Baronet, inheriting his father's fortune and banking firm, and Gatton Manor, Surrey. Sir George also served as MP for Arundel in 1754–74 and was influential in the East India Company, being elected as a director in 1767 and then chairman in 1769, 1770 and 1772. Colebrooke was known for his ostentation and speculative investments: during his tenure, the East India Company suffered financial collapse. Moreover, from 1771 several of his own investments brought major losses and his bank was forced to close in 1773. Gatton Manor was sold in 1777 and Colebrooke was declared bankrupt. He retired to Boulogne in 1778 and lived on a modest pension of £200 per annum which he had been voted by the East India Company. By 1789, however, Sir George had returned to live in Bath, having paid off his creditors and with a portion of his property salvaged.[326] There is no evidence, however, that he returned to Arlington Street.

In 1771 – the year that Sir George's financial woes began – he commissioned Adam to install a new interior at 23 Arlington Street. By then he was well known to the Adams, having lent them money on mortgage to help fund the construction of Chandos House (see p. 56).[327] Presumably the Arlington Street project was begun before Sir George's investments began to fail, or at the least before he realised how serious the situation had become. Surviving at the Soane Museum are designs for at least seven rooms, as well as a selection of furniture. The existence of ceiling designs for the front parlour and back parlour suggest that the house was arranged as a typical terraced house, with large rooms to the front and rear. A ceiling design for a saloon-cum-drawing room is inscribed *Cieling for the back room one pair Story at Sir George Colebrooke's in Arlington Street*, directing us to the rear first-floor room above the back parlour (Fig. 85). Moreover, there are designs for a gallery or library, the shape and scale of which suggest that this room was intended to span an entire wing at the rear of the house (Fig. 86), and the inclusion of French sash doors indicate its location at ground-floor level.

---

[324] Harris, 2007, p. 143. Weinreb, 2008, p. 26.
[325] Bradley, 2003, p. 602.
[326] HoP: George Colebrooke: http://www.historyofparliamentonline.org/volume/1754-1790/member/colebrooke-george-1729-1809 (accessed 5/08/2016). ODNB: Sir George Colebrooke: http://www.oxforddnb.com/view/article/37301?docPos=1 (accessed 5/08/2016).
[327] London Metropolitan Archives, Middlesex Deeds Registry 1770/2/40.

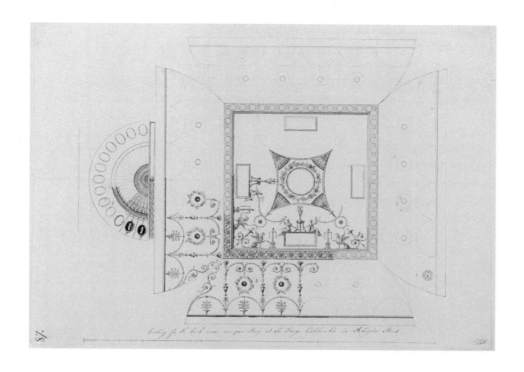

Fig 85. Adam office, design for a ceiling for the saloon at 23 Arlington Street, 1771. SM Adam volume 12/87. Photograph: Ardon Bar-Hama

Fig 86. Adam office, design for a ceiling for the gallery at 23 Arlington Street, 1771. SM Adam volume 12/82. Photograph: Ardon Bar-Hama

There is no evidence that any of Adam's designs for Sir George were executed in full; indeed, it is unlikely that he would have had the funds to proceed. However, on one design for the ceiling of the saloon-cum-drawing room, there is a pencil inscription in the hand of Adam's Italian draughtsman Joseph Bonomi: *1771 – Cominciato questo Lavoro* [1771 – begun this work]; this suggests that the work was at least started, and then presumably abandoned at some time shortly thereafter.[328] Little is known of 23 Arlington Street as the house had been demolished by the time Arthur Bolton wrote his two-volume study of the Adam brothers in 1922.[329] In this instance, Adam's surviving drawings are the only means of understanding Sir George's ambitions for the house. Its site is now occupied by a 1960s office block erected behind the Ritz Hotel.

Dover Street

Running north from the centre of Piccadilly, Dover Street was developed in the seventeenth century and named after Henry Jermyn, Baron Dover. Today very few of the buildings on Dover Street pre-date the nineteenth century.[330]

19 (later 30) Dover Street

No. 19 was located on the west side of Dover Street, set back from the road.[331] The house is little known, but it was the London home of John Ashburnham, 2nd Earl of Ashburnham, who succeeded to his father's Earldom in 1737. In 1756 he married Elizabeth Crawley, the daughter of Alderman John Crawley, a wealthy London merchant, from whom she inherited £200,000.[332]

In 1773 Ashburnham commissioned Adam to make alterations at 19 Dover Street, including interior decoration and a new screen and entrance gates.[333] In the Soane Museum are 37 surviving drawings for this work. Adam's design for the screen is not dated, but it shows a central porter's lodge ornamented with a blind relieving arch enclosing the Ashburnham arms, and surmounted by an urn and armorial hounds; the lodge is flanked to either side by double wooden gates with glass lamps on top of each gate pier (Fig. 87). The scheme was executed with sculpted hounds supplied by George Eckstein and the lodge appears on a map of 1813.[334]

Adam's designs for the house's interior decoration include ceilings, chimneypieces, mirror frames and a small but ornate library with bookcases set into the walls (Fig. 88). All of these are in Adam's characteristic neoclassical style, but as the house no longer survives and there is no known photographic evidence, it is not known how many of his designs were executed.

[328] SM Adam volume 12/86.
[329] Bolton, 1922, Volume II, Index p. 34.
[330] Weinreb, 2008, pp. 245-46.
[331] King, 2001, Volume 1, p. 296.
[332] J. Ingamells, *A dictionary of British and Irish travellers in Italy, 1701-1800*, 1997, p. 30.
[333] Colvin, 2008, p. 50.
[334] King, 2001, Volume 1, p. 298.

Fig 87. Adam office, design for a screen and entrance gates for 19 Dover Street, *c*.1773. SM Adam volume 51/45. Photograph: Ardon Bar-Hama

However, according to David King the existence of designs for minute details such as door furniture suggest that the scheme progressed far enough for at least some of Adam's proposals to have come to fruition. Moreover, some ceiling designs are inscribed as being incorrect or unused, suggesting that other schemes were executed. The house was demolished *c*.1910 and Adam's screen was probably taken down around the same time.[335]

[335] Ibid.

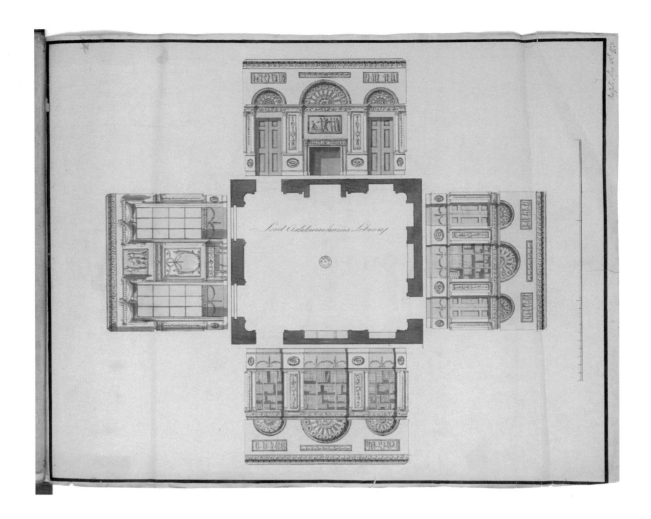

Fig 88. Adam office, design for the library at 19 Dover Street, 1773. SM Adam volume 50/8. Photograph: Ardon Bar-Hama

Pall Mall

Tradition has it that Pall Mall takes its name from the Italian ball game *pallo a maglio* played by Charles II in St James's Park: in order to prevent clouds of dust from passing carriages obscuring the game, the nearby thoroughfare was moved to its current location in 1661.[336] It was always a fashionable residential street, probably owing to its proximity to St James's Palace, and by the eighteenth century it was also the location of various clubs and shops.[337]

[336] SoL, Volume XX, 1940, chapter 8.
[337] Weinreb, 2008, pp. 620-21.

Carlton House

On the south side of the east end of Pall Mall, directly adjacent to St James's Park, Carlton House was built in 1709 for Henry Boyle, 1st Lord Carlton.[338] On his death in 1725 the house was inherited by his nephew, the 3rd Earl of Burlington, whose mother sold it in 1732 to Frederick, Prince of Wales.[339] Alterations to the interior and gardens were designed by William Kent in 1735.[340] Following her son's accession as George III, Augusta, Dowager Princess of Wales commissioned Sir William Chambers to make further alterations and improvements to the house and these works were carried out in 1763–69, swallowing up the neighbouring house, which had belonged to George Bubb Doddington – Adam's patron at La Trappe, Hammersmith.[341]

In 1767, during the tenure of Princess Augusta, James Adam was commissioned to design an entrance screen and gateway ornamented with sculptures of past sovereigns (Fig. 89).[342]

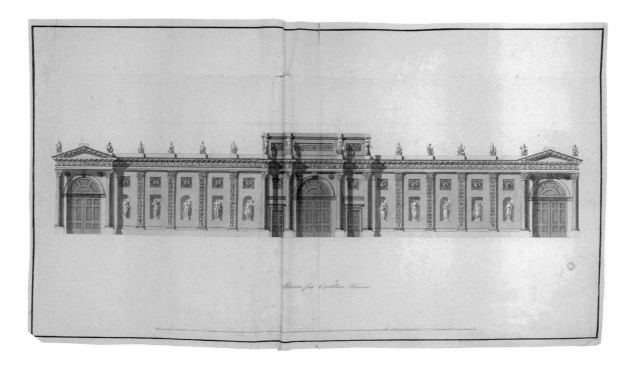

Fig 89. Adam office, design for a screen and gateway for Carlton House, 1776. SM Adam volume 29/1. Photograph: Ardon Bar-Hama

[338] Bradley, 2003, p. 439.
[339] Colvin, 1976, p. 138.
[340] Colvin, 2008, p. 617.
[341] Colvin, 1976, pp. 138-39.
[342] King, 2001, Volume 2, p. 202.

By these means the irregular front of Carlton House was to be concealed, but the design was not executed. According to the Adam brothers' preface to the first volume of their *Works in architecture…* (1773–78) the screen would have been made but for the Princess's failing health:

> *Design of a Gateway for Carleton House in Pall-Mall, done for her Royal Highness the late Princess Dowager of Wales. As the present court wall to Carleton House is extremely mean and irregular, her Royal Highness was desirous of remedying those defects, in such a manner as might render the approach to her town residence more proper and elegant. With this view the following design was formed, and considerable alterations were likewise proposed to be made upon the plan of the house itself: all of which were so much approved of by her Royal Highness, that she had determined to have carried them into execution, if the declining state of her heath had not prevented any steps from being taken towards the completion of this favourite plan.*[343]

James Adam's unexecuted design for Princess Augusta's screen is illustrated in the first volume of *Works in architecture…* but can also be seen in one surviving drawing at the Soane Museum.[344] It shows a triumphal arch gateway, flanked by links containing sculpture-filled niches, which are articulated by ornamented pilasters, and terminated at each end by a pedimented arched gate. The whole is ornamented with sculpture, including military trophies, portrait medallions and a frieze of festoons and arabesques.

George III gave Carlton House to his son, the Prince of Wales (later the Prince Regent) when he came of age in 1783.[345] This precipitated a large-scale and expensive series of works to designs by Henry Holland, who added a portico, an entrance screen, and remodelled the interior. The interior was further redecorated to designs by James Wyatt in the early nineteenth century and Wyatt also added another library and a strong room. At the same time a conservatory was added to designs by Thomas Hopper and John Nash made designs for remodelling the service quarters in the cellar.[346] However, when the Prince Regent became George IV he no longer required Carlton House and it was demolished from 1826.[347] A few chimneypieces were salvaged for Buckingham Palace, and the site was redeveloped as Carlton House Terrace to designs by Nash and James Pennethorne.[348] The terrace was badly damaged by bombing during the Second World War and while Nash's façades were restored, the interiors were largely altered.[349]

34 (later 25) Pall Mall

No. 34, on the north side of Pall Mall – with its rear elevation facing St James's Square – was the home of Andrew Millar, a bookseller, and a subscriber to Robert Adam's *Ruins of…*

---

[343] Adam, 1773-78, preface.
[344] Adam, 1773-78, part V, plate 1.
[345] Colvin, 1976, p. 139.
[346] Colvin, 2008, p. 529, 541, 736, 1189.
[347] H.M. Colvin, *The history of the King's works: 1782-1851*, Volume VI, 1973, pp. 321-22.
[348] Colvin, 2008, 734.
[349] Weinreb, 2008, p. 132.

Spalatro.[350] The son of a Renfrewshire clergyman, Millar acquired his first bookshop near St Clement's Church on the Strand in 1728 from a former employer, James McEuen, for whom Millar had sold Scotch Bibles. In 1748 he moved to better premises opposite the end of Katherine Street. He is known to have published the work of Henry Fielding, Samuel Johnson's great dictionary, James Thomson's *Seasons*, David Hume and William Robertson's volumes on the history of England and even Robert Adam's print of his design for the Admiralty screen at Whitehall (see p. 8).[351] Moreover, with the assistance of Patrick Murdock, Millar organised the publication of James Thomson's collected works in order to fund a funerary monument to Thomson, designed by Adam in 1762 for Poets' Corner in Westminster Abbey (see p. 12).[352]

In 1764 the bookshop was turned over to one of Millar's three apprentices, Thomas Caldwell, and during his retirement Millar rebuilt his house at 34 Pall Mall in 1765–66, to designs by Adam.[353] Millar first appears in the ratebooks for this area in December 1766, and remained at the house until his death in 1768.[354] As none of his three children survived infancy, on his death the house and Millar's £60,000 fortune were inherited by his wife, Jane Johnson, the

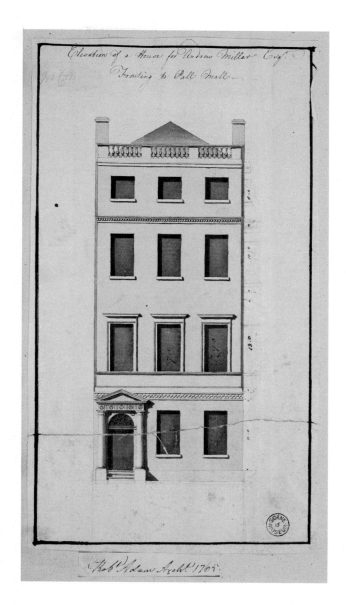

Fig 90. Adam office, design for the façade of 34 Pall Mall, 1765. SM Adam volume 46//15. Photograph: Ardon Bar-Hama

[350] ODNB: Andrew Millar: http://www.oxforddnb.com/view/article/18714?docPos=1 (accessed 5/08/2016). R. Adam, *Ruins of the Palace of the Emperor Diocletian at Spalatro in Dalmatia*, 1764, list of subscribers.
[351] ODNB: Andrew Millar.
[352] ODNB: James Thomson: http://www.oxforddnb.com/view/article/27306?docPos=2 (accessed 23/08/2016).
[353] ODNB: Andrew Millar.
[354] SoL, Volume XXIX, 1960, p. 326.

1766.

Ceiling of the Front Drawing room at Andrew Millar Esqr House
in Pall Mall.

Fig 91. Adam office, design for a ceiling for the front drawing room at 34 Pall Mall, 1766. SM Adam volume 11/173. Photograph: Ardon Bar-Hama

daughter of a Westminster print seller whom he had married in 1730. Jane went on to marry Sir Archibald Grant in 1780.[355]

At the Soane Museum there is a collection of eleven drawings for 34 Pall Mall. Seven of them show the fabric of the house as executed, being a relatively modest three-bay terraced house of four floors over a basement (Fig. 90). Four drawings show the neoclassical ceilings and chimneypieces for the front and back drawing rooms on the first floor (Fig. 91). These internal fittings are thought to have been executed in accordance with Adam's designs, but the house has since been demolished and there is no photographic evidence of its interiors.

During the 1820s the house was occupied by John Gibson Lockhart, the son-in-law of Sir Walter Scott, and in the 1830s by John Macdonald, the Adjutant General of Horse Guards.

It was later demolished, at an unknown date.[356] Its plot is now one half of a large 1930s office building which spans Nos 25 and 26 Pall Mall, facing St James's Square on the other side.

[355] ODNB: Andrew Millar.
[356] SoL, Volume XXIX, 1960, p. 326.

Cumberland House

No. 86 Pall Mall was originally known as York House, being a brick Palladian house built in 1761–63 to designs by Matthew Brettingham the elder for Prince Edward Augustus, Duke of York and Albany, the brother of George III.[357] Brettingham's house is illustrated in the fourth volume of *Vitruvius Britannicus*.[358] When the Duke of York died in 1767 the house passed first to his brother Prince William Henry, Duke of Gloucester and Edinburgh, and then in 1772 to his youngest brother, Prince Henry Frederick, Duke of Cumberland and Strathearn: hence it came to be known as Cumberland House.[359]

The young duke was a colourful character. His family did not credit him with intellectual prowess, and he was given few of the responsibilities shouldered by his older brothers. In 1766 he became Ranger of Windsor Forest and Great Park, and in 1768 entered the navy as a midshipman, being promoted to Rear-Admiral only a year later, Vice-Admiral in 1770 and Admiral of the White in 1782. However, Cumberland is not remembered for his naval career but for his romantic dalliances, first with the wife of the 1st Earl of Grosvenor – Adam's patron at Eaton Hall. In 1770 Cumberland was obliged to borrow money from his brother the King in order to pay £10,000 in damages to Lord Grosvenor, following a trial for 'criminal conversation' with Lady Grosvenor.[360]

In 1771 Cumberland married Anne Luttrell, the daughter of Simon Luttrell, Baron Irnham, and widow of Mr Christopher Horton, who had died two years previously.[361] Horace Walpole described Anne as follows: 'The new Princess of the Blood is a young widow of twenty-four, extremely pretty, not handsome, very well made, with the most amorous eyes in the world, and eyelashes a yard long. Coquette beyond measure, artful as Cleopatra, and completely mistress of all her passions and projects.'[362] George III disapproved of the marriage as he did not consider Anne a suitable bride for a king's brother: although the daughter of a Baron, she was a 'commoner' and therefore any child born of the marriage would not be a legitimate heir to the Electorate of Hanover. As a result Cumberland and Anne were exiled from court and in 1772 the Royal Marriages Act was passed to safeguard the royal line from dilution or the threat of an unstable succession. The Act prescribed the legal terms under which any descendant of George II could marry and a strict right of veto was vested in the sovereign. Unfortunately, this forced Cumberland's brother, the Duke of Gloucester, to admit his secret six-year marriage to the equally unsuitable Dowager Countess of Waldegrave, the illegitimate daughter of Sir Edward Walpole.[363]

The Cumberlands were not reconciled with the King for almost a decade and Anne was never received at court. They spent much of their time on the Continent, but when in Britain

---

[357] Ibid., p. 364.

[358] J. Woolfe and J. Gandon, *Vitruvius Britannicus*, Volume IV, 1767, pl. 5-7.

[359] SoL, Volume XXIX, 1960, p. 365.

[360] ODNB: Henry Frederick, Prince, Duke of Cumberland and Strathearn: http://www.oxforddnb.com/view/article/12963?docPos=4 (accessed 5/08/2016).

[361] Ibid.

[362] Yale Edition, *Horace Walpole's Correspondence*, Volume 23, p. 345: http://images.library.yale.edu/hwcorrespondence/page.asp (accessed 5/08/2016).

[363] ODNB: Duke of Cumberland.

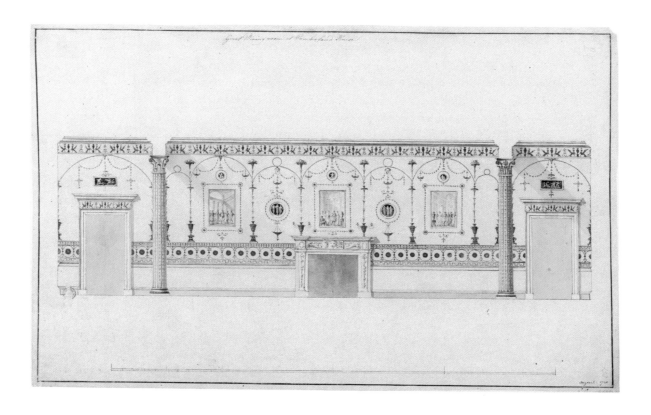

Fig 92. Adam office, design for the chimney wall of the great dining room at Cumberland House, 1780. SM Adam volume 14/138. Photograph: Ardon Bar-Hama

they lived either in Brighton or at Cumberland House.[364] Until his death in 1790, Cumberland persistently sought to improve the house, largely with the aid of Adam.[365] It has been suggested that these enhancements were made to produce a social alternative to the royal court, in which the Cumberlands could ignore the King and entertain their own social circle. This circle included Anne's sister Elizabeth, later a resident at Cumberland House, who was badly behaved and vulgar. She was also a gambling thief, convicted of pick-pocketing in Augsburg, and eventually poisoned herself, having descended to a penniless street-sweeper. Also part of this social circle was Anne's aunt, the Dowager Countess of Home – an Adam patron at Home House in Portman Square – famously known as 'The Queen of Hell' for her lavish social entertainments (see p. 59).[366]

In 1781 Adam made designs for altering the music room on the ground floor, adding a new ceiling which survived until the demolition of the house in the early twentieth century. Adam

[364] Ibid.
[365] SoL, Volume XXIX, 1960, p. 365.
[366] ODNB: Duke of Cumberland.

Fig 93. Adam office, design for the window wall of the third drawing room at Cumberland House, *c.*1780–85. SM Adam volume 49/19. Photograph: Ardon Bar-Hama

also introduced a lavish new great dining room, adjacent to the music room, which he created by knocking together two of Brettingham's original rooms. Adam's Etruscan-style ceiling for this room was executed, although it was gone by the time the house was demolished (Fig. 92).[367] Unexecuted designs for Cumberland House include a small private eating room on the ground floor, an oval boudoir for Anne in what had been Brettingham's state dressing room, and three magnificent drawing rooms on the first floor (Fig. 93). In addition, in 1785 Adam produced plans for a new wing, including a private apartment for Anne's dissolute sister Elizabeth, but this was not executed (Fig. 94).

The Duke of Cumberland died from an ulcerated lung in 1790 as he stepped from his carriage outside Cumberland House. Anne was awarded an annual allowance of £4,000 but being encumbered by her husband's debts was forced to sell Cumberland House to her bankers

[367] Stillman, 1966, pp. 78, 106.

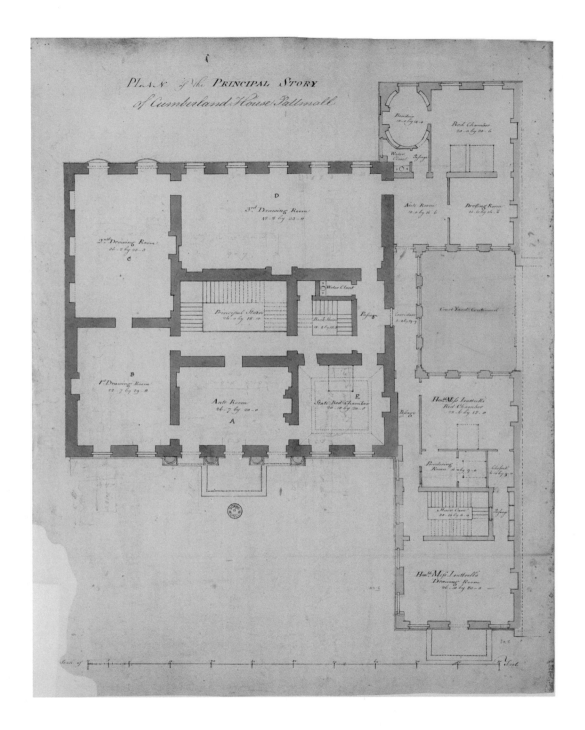

Fig 94. Adam office, plan showing a proposed extension to Cumberland House, 1785. SM Adam volume
49/15. Photograph: Ardon Bar-Hama

for £20,000 in 1793.[368] In 1807 the building was taken on by the Ordnance Office, later the War Office, and after years of neglect under that usage it was demolished between 1908 and 1911.[369] The site – and its neighbours – were then acquired by the Royal Automobile Club, who erected their building, with a 228 foot-wide Portland stone frontage built to designs by Messrs Mewès and Davis which remains *in situ*.[370]

Haymarket Opera House

At the southern end of Haymarket, at the corner with Pall Mall, Sir John Vanbrugh in 1704–5 built an opera house known as the King's/Queen's Theatre (depending on the monarch).[371] This burnt down in 1789 and Adam's schemes for its replacement, although undated, are doubtless from that period (Fig. 95).[372] One of Adam's patrons, the Hon. George Hobart, had held a half

Fig 95. Adam office, design for the Haymarket Opera House, *c*.1789. SM Adam volume 47/7. Photograph: Geremy Butler

368 ODNB: Duke of Cumberland.
369 Weinreb, 2008, p. 1036.
370 Bradley, 2003, p. 615.
371 Colvin, 2008, p. 1072.
372 King, 2001, Volume 2, p. 49.

share in the theatre until his retirement in 1773 (see 33 St James's Square, p. 139) but as Adam's plans appear to postdate Hobart's tenure, they were presumably drawn up as a speculation. Adam's vast scheme covered an extended plot and his drawings at the Soane Museum show that he proposed including an opera house, assembly rooms and tavern, with a multi-block elevation – complete with a *porte cochère* and separate entrances for the King and Queen – rippling with tripartite windows, domes and pediments. This ambitious rebuilding proposal was not executed, and instead a new opera house was built to designs by Michael Novosielski in 1790–91, with later work by John Nash.[373] It suffered a fire in 1867 and was demolished in the 1890s.[374]

St James's Square

Across Pall Mall from St James's Park, St James's Square was developed by Henry Jermyn, 1st Earl of St Albans, the great politician who served as Lord Chancellor to Charles II following the Restoration in 1660. Owing to its proximity to St James's Palace, during the seventeenth and eighteenth centuries, St James's Square became one of London's most fashionable and aristocratic addresses.[375]

11 St James's Square

A large townhouse – the largest in the square – was erected on its north side in the 1670s, immediately west of Duke of York Street. It served as the principal London residence of the Earl of St Albans until 1682, when he sold it to the 1st Duke of Ormonde. Here Nos 9-11 were built in 1735–6 as a speculative development by the builder Benjamin Timbrell, with assistance in design from the architect Henry Flitcroft.[376]

No. 11 is a four-storey, five-bay terraced house. Purchased from Timbrell by the Earl of Macclesfield for £6,150, it was later sold in 1766 by the Earl's widow to two merchants, Alexander Nesbitt and Hugh Hammersley, who within weeks passed it on to Sir Rowland Winn, 5th Baronet, of Nostell.[377] Sir Rowland had inherited the family estate of Nostell Priory near Wakefield on his father's death in 1765.[378] He married Sabine Louise, the daughter of Jacques Philippe, Baron d'Hervert, the Governor of Vevey, when he was only nineteen years old, having met and fallen in love with this older – and already married – lady while on his Grand Tour.[379] For just eight months he served as MP for Pontefract during 1768, only to be unseated following a petition prompted by his supporters having prevented opposing voters

[373] Colvin, 2008, pp. 732, 754.
[374] King, 2001, Volume 2, p. 50.
[375] Weinreb, 2008, p. 770.
[376] SoL, Volume XXIX, 1960, pp. 118, 122.
[377] Ibid., pp. 123-24.
[378] HoP: Sir Rowland Winn, 5th Baronet: http://www.historyofparliamentonline.org/volume/1754-1790/member/winn-sir-rowland-1739-85 (accessed 28/07/2016).
[379] Todd, 2005, pp. 205-8.

from reaching the poll.[380] Sir Rowland's other great achievement was his position as one of Adam's longest standing patrons.

Sir Rowland's father, the 4th Baronet, began replacing the original monastic buildings at Nostell from *c*.1736 with a large neo-Palladian house, designed by Colonel James Moyser and James Paine.[381] After his father's death, Sir Rowland dismissed Paine in favour of the more fashionable Adam, whom he employed there until his own death twenty years later.[382] Furthermore, Sir Rowland purchased his smart London townhouse at 11 St James's Square. As at Nostell, Thomas Chippendale was employed to furnish its interior but it was not until 1774 that Adam was commissioned to make alterations to the façade.[383]

Adam provided two alternative designs to reface the townhouse, but only those for the executed scheme survive, with the work carried out in 1774–76 (Fig. 96). As in Adam's drawing the new façade was executed with a rusticated basement with a Doric porch, and a three-bay portico of Adam's Spalatro order pilasters – the most characteristically Adam-style element of the design – which were unfortunately refitted with Corinthian capitals during the nineteenth century.[384] On this façade Adam made the first use of his infamous patented Liardet's stucco composition which invariably dropped off after twenty or thirty years.[385]

Contemporary correspondence within the family archive at the West Yorkshire Archive Service records that £6,930 was paid to the widowed Lady Sabine Winn by Christie's when 11 St James's Square was sold within a month of Sir Rowland's unexpected death in a carriage accident in 1785.[386] His son, the 6th Baronet was still a child of nine and the sale of the house was presumably hurried to alleviate the financial difficulties caused by Sir Rowland's political ambitions and protracted building works at Nostell. Indeed, Adam's final account of £247 15s 5d for work at Nostell remained unpaid for three years until September 1788, when he was obliged to write and remind Lady Winn of her obligation.[387] 11 St James's Square was purchased by the Hoare family but only occasionally used until 1798 when it was occupied for nineteen years by Alexander Davidson, the collector of British paintings and Nelson's prize agent, and later, in the early twentieth century it was the London home of Lord Iveagh who rescued Kenwood and bequeathed it to the nation.[388]

Adam's elevation at 11 St James's Square survives relatively well. Minor alterations made in the 1870s by Messrs Trollope and Sons were removed during restoration work in 1988-91 by the Thomas Saunders Partnership, including the Corinthian capitals. The house now contains offices (Fig. 97), while Timbrell's other two houses in this block (Nos 9 and 10) accommodate the Royal Institute of International Affairs.[389]

---

[380] HoP: Sir Rowland Winn, 5th Baronet.
[381] Colvin, 2008, pp. 713, 769.
[382] Ibid., p. 51.
[383] Ibid., pp. 50, 199.
[384] King, 2001, Volume 1, p. 290.
[385] Bradley, 2003, p. 627.
[386] WYAS WYL1352(1) A1/5A/10.
[387] WYAS WYL1352(1) A4/1551/1.
[388] SoL, Volume XXIX, 1960, p. 124.
[389] Bradley, 2003, p. 627.

Fig 96. Adam office, design for the façade of 11 St James's Square, 1774. SM Adam volume 41/49.
Photograph: Ardon Bar-Hama

Fig 97. 11 St James's Square 2016. Photograph: Lewis Bush

20 St James's Square

Little is known of the original seventeenth-century house built at 20 St James's Square, which first appeared in the Westminster ratebooks in 1675. In 1771 the freeholder, the 1st Earl Bathurst, acquired an Act of Parliament allowing him to break an entail on the property. Bathurst sold the house for £18,500 to a wealthy Welshman, Sir Watkin Williams Wynn, 4th Baronet, of Wynnstay.[390] Sir Watkin had succeeded his father in 1749 when he was only five months old and his long minority coupled with income from vast landholdings resulted in an accumulation of great wealth.[391] In 1769 he married Lady Henrietta Somerset, the fifth daughter of Charles, 4th Duke of Beaufort, but she died the same year, and in 1771 he married again, Charlotte Grenville, the daughter of the Hon. George Grenville, sister of the Marquess of Buckingham, and aunt of the 1st Duke of Buckingham. It was following this second marriage that Sir Watkin acquired 20 St James's Square. Although he served as MP for Shropshire in 1772–74 and Denbighshire in 1774–78, Sir Watkin was not the powerful and determined politician that his father had been, pursuing instead a deep interest in art, music and theatre.[392] Indeed, at his country home of Wynnstay House, Denbighshire, he built a private theatre in 1771–72 to designs by James Gandon (demolished in 1858).[393]

On acquiring 20 St James's Square, Sir Watkin immediately demolished the original house, commissioning designs for rebuilding from James Gandon, from whom he had received lessons in architecture.[394] However, it was the more fashionable Robert Adam who won the commission and his designs were built in 1772–75.[395] There are over 80 surviving Adam office drawings for 20 St James's Square at the Soane Museum, including designs for the house itself, a screen in the garden, ceilings, walls, friezes, chimneypieces, glass frames, furniture, door furniture, door panels, plate and a sedan chair for urban use by Lady Williams Wynn (Fig. 98). The craftsmen who worked on the house included the mason John Devall, the plasterer Joseph Rose, the painter Antonio Zucchi and John Hinchcliff, who provided the marble chimneypieces, with an estimated total cost for the building and its furnishings standing at a little over £29,000.[396]

The building is a three-storey, three-bay terraced house, set behind area railings, with a rusticated ground floor containing relieving arches over the door and windows (Fig. 99). Above, the bays are articulated by giant Corinthian pilasters which range across both the first and second floors, and the windows on the first floor are pedimented, set within relieving arches and behind balconies. The plan of 20 St James's Square is often compared to Adam's earlier Chandos House (see p. 56), with a suite of interconnecting parade rooms, illustrating that the house was intended principally for entertaining (Fig. 100). The entrance hall gives access to the stairwell and the first floor, where there is a route comprising an ante-room, front drawing room and rear drawing room – with the front and rear drawing rooms subtly connected by

[390] SoL, Volume XXIX, 1960, p. 164. J. Stourton, *Great houses of London*, 2012, p. 94.
[391] Harris, 2001, p. 257.
[392] HoP: Sir Watkin Williams Wynn: http://www.historyofparliamentonline.org/volume/1754-1790/member/wynn-sir-watkin-williams-1748-89 (accessed 17/08/2016).
[393] Colvin, 2008, p. 404.
[394] SoL, Volume XXIX, 1960, p. 164.
[395] Colvin, 2008, p. 49.
[396] SoL, Volume XXIX, 1960, p. 164.

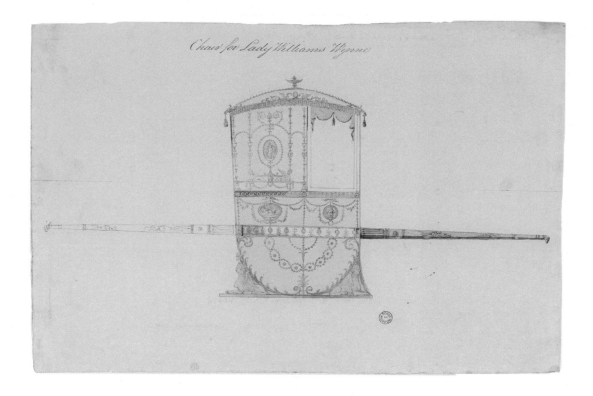

Fig 98. Adam office, design for a sedan chair for 20 St James's Square, *c.*1773–5. SM Adam volume 49/39.
Photograph: Ardon Bar-Hama

seamlessly united apsidal ends. In the rear wing was Lady Williams Wynn's dressing room and private apartment, which could be added to the circuit for larger entertainments. On the ground floor a front dining room was connected by apsidal ends to a music room behind, with Sir Watkin's library and private apartment in the rear wing beyond.

The interior decoration at 20 St James's Square is particularly lavish and all in the neoclassical style. Both first-floor drawing rooms have decorative plasterwork ceilings, that to the rear in the form of an elaborate and colourful compartmental barrel vault, and each room has a carved marble chimneypiece, that in the front room being clearly inspired by a plate from Giovanni Battista Piranesi's recently published *Diverse maniere d'adornare i cammini* (1769) (Fig. 101).[397] Perhaps the most intimate Adam interior was Lady Williams Wynn's 'semi-public' dressing room (Fig. 102). Here Adam prevented the rectangular room from feeling like a corridor by cleverly dividing the space into three portions, with barrel vaults over the end units and a groin vault in the centre. The scheme was completed with a Venetian window, bookcases and

[397] Harris, 2001, p. 260.

Fig 99. Adam office, design for the façade of 20 St James's Square, 1771–72. SM Adam volume 40/65.
Photograph: Ardon Bar-Hama

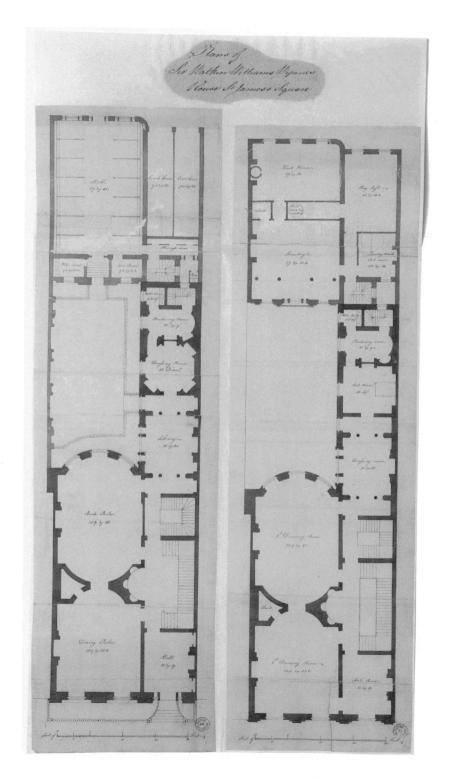

Fig 100. Adam office, plan showing the ground and first floors of 20 St James's Square, 1771–72. SM Adam volumes 40/66-67. Photograph: Ardon Bar-Hama

Fig 101. Adam office, design for a chimneypiece for the front drawing room at 20 St James's Square, 1772. SM Adam volume 23/10. Photograph: Ardon Bar-Hama

an Adam chimneypiece with inlaid scagliola and Wedgwood basalt tablets (Sir Watkin was one of Wedgwood's most faithful patrons).[398] Unfortunately, the Wedgwood elements of the chimneypiece have since been replaced with replicas.[399]

On the ground floor, the inclusion of a music room was unusual in a terraced-house arrangement. However, Sir Watkin was particularly keen on music, spending around £300 per annum on musical instruments and lessons.[400] The centrepiece was an organ made by John Snetzler, with a case designed by Adam, which included muse terms representing Euterpe and Terpsichore – similar to the organ case Adam had designed for Kedleston Hall in 1765 – and a medallion of Handel.[401] The organ and its Adam case were removed from 20 St James's Square in 1864 and are now in the National Museum of Wales, Cardiff.

The Wynn family kept 20 St James's Square as their principal London residence until 1906, when at first it was leased to the Earl Strathmore, father to the Queen Mother, and then the freehold was sold to the Eagle Star Insurance Company.[402] In 1935 it was sold again to the Distillers' Company who had, the year before, purchased and rebuilt the neighbouring house at No. 21 in sympathy with Adam's façade to designs by Mewès and Davis.[403] Happily, the Adam interiors at No. 20 were preserved but at the same time the house was extended upwards by two floors.[404] This however, is less intrusive than it might be, as the new third floor is set behind Adam's roofline balustrade and the fourth floor is a mansard roof. In 2009 the freehold of both

[398] Harris, 2007, p. 161.
[399] Harris, 2001, p. 266.
[400] Ibid., p. 269.
[401] SoL, Volume XXIX, 1960, p. 168.
[402] Stourton, 2012, p. 98.
[403] Weinreb, 2008, p. 772.
[404] Bradley, 2003, p. 631.

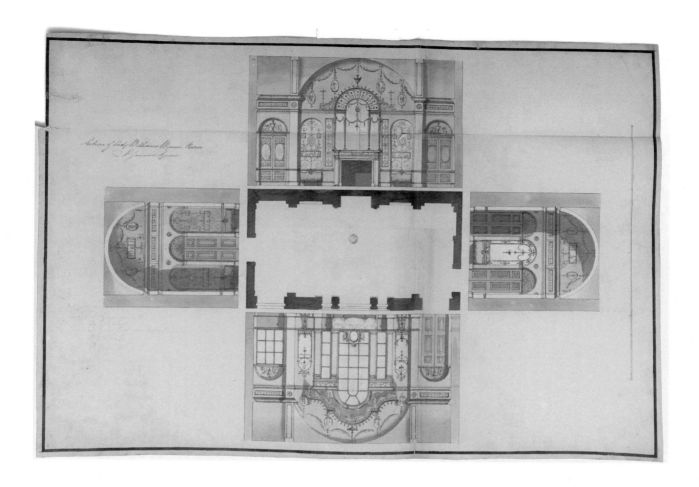

Fig 102. Adam office, design for Lady Williams Wynn's dressing room at 20 St James's Square, *c.*1772. SM Adam volume 40/70. Photograph: Ardon Bar-Hama

buildings were acquired by an IT company, and this year No. 20 has been sold again to a private individual who reportedly plans to convert the building back to domestic use.[405]

33 St James's Square

Like 20 St James's Square, little is known of the seventeenth-century house at No. 33 on the east side of the square, although it first appeared in ratebooks in 1673 and was purchased by the 1st Earl of Buckingham in 1734.[406] In 1770–72 it was entirely rebuilt and decorated for the Hon.

[405] Stourton, 2012, p. 98.
[406] SoL, Volume XXIX, 1960, p. 206.

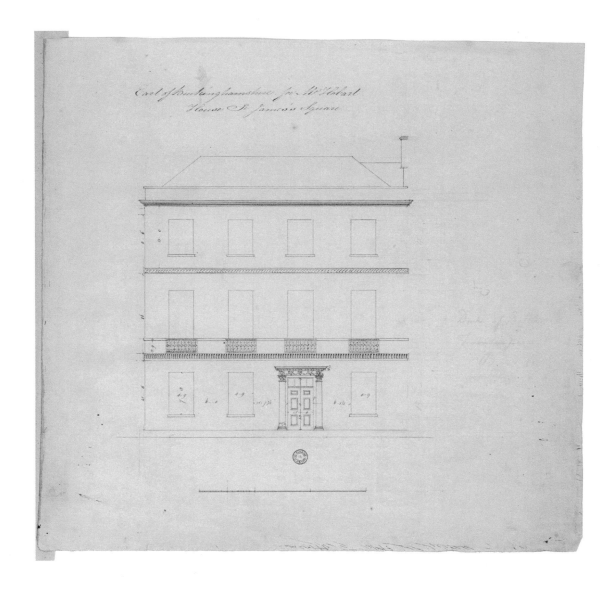

Fig 103. Adam office, design for the façade of 33 St James's Square, 1770. SM Adam volume 44/14.
Photograph: Ardon Bar-Hama

George Hobart to designs by Adam as a relatively unadorned, L-shaped, three-storey, four-bay house, facing the square, and with a very plain seven-bay north side on Charles II Street.

George Hobart was the fourth son of the 1st Earl of Buckinghamshire. Despite a lengthy political career during which he served as MP for St Ives, Cornwall in 1754–61 and Bere Alston, Devon in 1761–80, he held aspirations to a career in the diplomatic service. He even travelled to St Petersburg in 1762 to work as secretary to his half-brother John Hobart, 2nd Earl

Fig 104. Adam office, design for a ceiling for the front drawing room at 33 St James's Square, 1770. SM Adam volume 12/39. Photograph: Ardon Bar-Hama

of Buckinghamshire's Embassy to Catherine the Great, but this was not a successful posting as Hobart found the Moscow climate too bleak and within a year had returned to Britain. Further to these public works Hobart was also a great lover of opera and on his return to Britain became manager of the King's Theatre, Haymarket, purchasing a half-share in the theatre in 1769. He transformed it into a successful commercial enterprise and maintained his personal financial stake until 1773 when he retired, reputedly because of 'financial strain'.[407]

One may wonder, therefore, how Hobart could afford to rebuild his townhouse, especially considering the burden of his famously obese wife Albinia, whom he had married in 1757. After producing nine children, the couple usually lived separately, but she was a gambler and opened her house, Nocton Hall on Ham Common (inherited by Hobart from a distant relative

[407] HoP: George Hobart, 3rd Earl of Buckinghamshire: http://www.historyofparliamentonline.org/volume/1754-1790/member/hobart-hon-george-1731-1804 (accessed 28/07/20116). ODNB: George Hobart, 3rd Earl of Buckinghamshire: http://www.oxforddnb.com/view/article/13390 (accessed 28/07/2016).

in 1766), twice a week for gaming. Moreover, Hobart's financial difficulties were not alleviated when he succeeded to his half-brother's Earldom in 1793, as this inheritance did not include the family estates which the 2nd Earl had divided between his daughters.[408]

A clue as to how the house was funded can be found on one of Adam's surviving drawings, where an inscription reads: *Earl of Buckinghamshire for Mr Hobart / House St James's Square* (Fig. 103). This suggests that 33 St James's Square was rebuilt for Hobart at the behest and cost of his brother. The truth of this is unknown, but most of Adam's surviving designs for the house were executed, resulting in a simple but pleasant building with a modest Corinthian door to the square and pretty ironwork balconettes to the first-floor windows. Adam also installed some beautiful interiors, for which the drawings survive. Three colourful Adam-style ceilings remain in situ – in the front drawing room overlooking the square (Fig. 104); in the adjacent dressing room (which has now been knocked together with the front drawing room); and in the rear drawing room. There is also an attractive Adam chimneypiece in the front drawing room with volute stiles surmounted by ram masks.

The house was inherited in 1804 by Hobart's son, the 4th Earl of Buckinghamshire, and sold a year later for £11,100 to the 2nd Lord Eliot (later 1st Earl St Germans).[409] Eliot commissioned substantial alterations and extensions at the rear to designs by Sir John Soane, which were carried out intermittently between 1805 and 1823.[410] In 1855–69 the house belonged to the 14th Earl of Derby, Prime Minister in 1852, 1858–59 and 1866–68, and a fourth floor was added to the house in the 1870s by his son, the 15th Earl of Derby.[411] Derby then sold the building in 1910 for £54,000 to the English and Scottish Law Assurance Association, who a year later undertook further works, including the addition of a stone balcony, stone facings to the ground floor, a mansard roof, and various alterations to the interior, all to designs by Messrs Edmerton and Gabriel.[412] The house was remodelled in 1999 resulting in the loss of the Soane interiors, which were removed in favour of replica Adam interiors. The building is now used as offices.

---

[408] Ibid.
[409] SoL, Volume XXIX, 1960, p. 207.
[410] Colvin, 2008, p. 970.
[411] Bradley, 2003, p. 633.
[412] SoL, Volume XXIX, 1960, p. 209.